THE ILLUSTRATED BOOK OF

architects and architecture

THE ILLUSTRATED BOOK OF

architects and architecture

edited by

Mike Darton

TIGER BOOKS INTERNATIONAL
LONDON

A QUINTET BOOK

This edition first published 1990 by
Tiger Books International PLC
London

This book was designed and produced by
Quintet Publishing Limited
6 Blundell Street
London N7 9BH

Creative Director: Peter Bridgewater
Art Director: Ian Hunt
Designer: Stuart Walden, Nicki Simmonds
Project Editor: Mike Darton
Editor: Lindsay Porter

Typeset in Great Britain by
Central Southern Typesetters, Eastbourne
Manufactured in Hong Kong by
Regent Publishing Services Limited
Printed in Hong Kong by
Leefung-Asco Printers Limited

Some of the material in this book previously
appeared in *Twentieth Century Architecture,*
The Principles of Architecture and *The Architecture*
Source Book

contents

1 introduction

ARCHITECTURE IS ESSENTIALLY the art of reconciliation. It involves resolving specific and general demands of its users within a projected image of three-dimensional form.

The distinction between architecture as opposed to mere building is hard to define, perhaps easier to recognize. No doubt many of the humbler buildings of early times, structures long since destroyed, displayed much technological ingenuity and attractive decoration, but, like their counterparts in primitive societies today, their status as architecture or building must remain a matter of personal choice. The twin threads of abstract design and structural experiment act and interact in buildings of all epochs, sometimes in harmony, at other times one taking precedence for a period over the other.

A building, as an object that defines and encloses space, reflects the society of its time more than any other art-form. The meaning of any building is transmitted as much by the materials in which it is built as by the function it is designed to perform. The vast majority of buildings consist of external walls surrounding an interior space and covered by a roof to provide shelter. Their basic shape directly relates to the materials chosen to form that enclosure, and that choice reflects a relationship between the architect's attitude to design and the materials in which that design is executed.

■ materials and availability

Throughout the history of architecture, there has always been correspondence between the architect's attitude to space and the choice of materials used to define and articulate it. Abstract design parameters such as context, time, function and style must be matched to more obvious considerations, such as the availability and suitability of materials, climate and economy.

How available a material is, closely relates to cost: the further it needs to be transported, the more expensive it becomes and the less "available". With the growth of mass transportation, particularly in the nineteenth and twentieth centuries, materials could be moved from one side of the world to the other, but while the actual cost of doing so may be prohibitive, it may also be entirely inappropriate to remove a natural material from its geographical region. The expense of materials such as marble is partly to do with the real costs involved in its quarrying and transport, but it is also to do with market costs relating to demand and rarity value.

■ structure

The physical properties of different materials are also crucial. Masonry construction, piling heavy blocks of stone or brick on top of each other, makes a solid wall construction which encloses space and is also self-supporting.

On the other hand, the structural qualities of steel and timber have encouraged the development of frame systems in which the primary structure is made up of a skeleton of columns and beams, often made off site in a factory, which can then be clad in an entirely different weathering and insulating skin, made of either solid or transparent material. It is therefore hardly surprising that the type of buildings designed for twentieth-century needs have little precedent, either in function, form or constructional method.

Another type of construction for connecting spaces and for achieving a close relationship between the outside and the inside of a building also contrasts with the limitations of solid wall techniques, despite being an extension of that technique – concrete. Concrete is a material made by mixing a number of ingredients – cement, sand, stone aggregate and water – to make a slurry which can be poured into shaped moulds before it sets hard. It is consequently appropriate for both frame and solid wall structures, either made on site or prefabricated.

Apart from being capable of spanning large distances when combined with steel reinforcement, its most significant quality for twentieth-century architecture is its plasticity. Freed from the rectilinear constraints of building in some form of solid block, the architect has been able to make organic compositions of free-flowing and asymmetrical shapes. All this has come about through great advances in

RIGHT Geographical considerations play a large part in the materials and form of building. In Mediterranean countries whitewashed exteriors and small window openings help to keep interiors cool.

basic techniques: reinforcement has already been mentioned, but there are in addition considerable economic benefits in precasting and, especially, in prestressing. It is likely that careful and scientific experimentation will lead to further improvements.

ABOVE La Muralla Roja, Spain (1973, Ricardo Bofill). Here the building is itself a type of decoration, the bright sculptural form contrasting with the rugged setting.

■ geography

As well as considering the choice of materials in relation to a particular building type, the geological conditions of the ground on which the building will stand are important, particularly as far as weight and height are concerned. The rock base of New York City made the early skyscrapers realistic propositions, although the relatively crude methods for their construction relied on mass and weight for stability. The likelihood of earthquakes in Los Angeles or the clay soil conditions in London both dictate different attitudes to construction, which in turn influence the form and style of their architecture.

Climatic conditions dictate different constraints. In the tropics, the need for shade and natural ventilation, together with the problems of intervening rainy seasons, has led to a traditional architecture of large over-hanging roofs, with little weather-proofing on the walls beneath. On the other hand, the conditions in northern Europe, where there is relatively light, but continual, rainfall, without great extremes of temperature, call for entirely different techniques of weathering and insulation.

Finally, there are aspects of geography that are even more immediate: the actual surroundings of a proposed building, in terms of other buildings and structures adjacent to the site. In Europe in particular, over the past few decades, local planning authorities have been keen to promote the "blending in" of new buildings with those already existing: this may not be good for architectural progress, but it is a restraint to respect.

■ the role of the architect through history

Architecture is only possible among communities untroubled by persistent wars. It is among settled agrarian communities therefore that we find nurseries of the arts, and when such conditions are fortified by successful foreign trade, such as in Egypt and Greece, then the architectural results can be dramatic.

The earliest buildings that have survived, in the Middle East and particularly in Egypt, are mostly stone-built palaces and temples, structurally conservative but massively monumental, even oppressive. Their cost in human labour can only be imagined with a shudder: indeed how the common people and slaves lived must be left to the imagination or glimpsed in the cartoon-like images of wall paintings and ancient reliefs.

Little would have been known about the role of the architect before the Middle Ages had it not been for a relatively unknown Roman architect and engineer living in the first century BC. Vitruvius' *Ten Books on Architecture* survived every other contemporary work of the Greek and Roman Empires, and have remained a highly influential source in the development of Western architecture.

Greek architecture was the expression of a balanced community, in which the essential religious and civic institutions remained the stable ingredient. The architect was responsible for both the design and supervision of buildings in Ancient Greece and was recognized as essential in the development of that society. By Roman times the role of the architect had changed to that of technician and military engineer rather than artist.

Throughout history, the essential relationship of trust and understanding between patron, designer and builder has been critical to the realization of any building project, and in the Middle Ages it was more often the patron who was credited with the creation of a building. The great master-builders were by no means considered second-rate, but the idea of the artist as a designer did not exist. The building of the great medieval cathedrals and castles often took place over several generations, with successive master-builders adapting and adding to the building as it progressed rather than working to a preconceived design. In spite of their considerable technical skills, much of the work relied on trial-and-error, with each team learning from experience to push the techniques of their materials to new limits.

In Renaissance Italy, the importance of architectural literature as a means of transmitting ideas lost since

Classical times was reestablished and the architect was again elevated to the role of artist. The existence of architectural theory provided the literate amateur with a new awareness of building design which had previously been exlusive to the craft guilds, and the subsequent combination of the academic patron working closely with the practical surveyor or engineer was the basis for the later establishment of a profession.

Without the interest of such enlightened patrons as the Earl of Arundel, with whom Inigo Jones (1573–1652) visited Italy in 1613–1614, English Renaissance architecture would not have been established in the mainstream of European culture. Originally a masque designer to the Court of James I, it was only by studying actual buildings in Italy that Inigo Jones was able to understand fully the work of Sebastiano Serlio and Andrea Palladio (1508–80), previously only known from writings and plates, Jones returned to England in 1615, became Surveyor to the King, and established himself as the first English architect in the sense that we understand the term today.

Relative stability in society and a slow growth rate in the population over the next 200 years meant that architects remained primarily involved with royal, civic and institutional buildings and with urban planning.

ABOVE AND BELOW The Parthenon. It has been strongly suggested that most of the detailed shaping is a transformation in masonry of a style developed in timber construction.

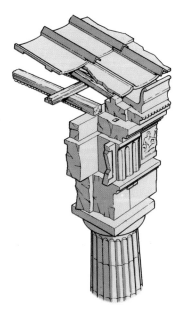

Following the severe depredations in urban architecture that resulted from the absolute materialism of the Industrial Revolution in England, a personal rather than social concern on the part of the growing middle classes at the destruction of the city prompted the reappearance of the architect as artist. Vested in the neo-Gothic stylistic revival of the nineteenth century was a belief in the truth, purity and simplicity of the society to which Gothic architecture originally belonged. This desire to return to what was understood to be the innate traditions of English architecture was also reflected in William Morris' Arts and Crafts Movement.

In the early part of this century, the architect as a formally trained individual emerged. More and more complicated environmental and constructional problems, and a rapidly expanding birth rate, promoted trends towards specialization in all sectors of society. Once a privileged position had been established, the architect, as with other professionals, began to throw up barriers to maintain status. It is only now that those barriers are beginning to come down again.

The specialist demands made on today's architect, who has to undergo a minimum of five years' formal training, are very close to Vitruvius' aspirations. Vitruvius said that architects should have imagination, an understanding of both theoretical and practical aspects of construction, should be versed in letters, drawing, the use of geometrical instruments, optics, arithmetic, history, philosophy, music, medicine, law and astronomy.

■ other historical influences

Architecture is subject to a good many influences other than the materials available or the contemporary style. Historical events, for example, may be just as significant. War, or the threat of war, has been responsible for many of the technical advances in solid construction rendered necessary by the need for tenable defence. Similarly, the rituals and practice of religion may require its own architectural style in building. Thus a Christian church is generally in the shape of a cross, a mosque has an associated minaret from which the faithful can be called to prayer, and so on.

Such styles are more than national because they represent more than national interests. In terms of defensive architecture, every planner intends to follow the latest proven advances, and certainly to imitate an enemy thought to have devised a more advantageous form of defence. The effects of religious architecture are transferred just as directly, but more often by actual conquest. The religious architecture of southern Spain, for instance, was entirely transmuted by the occupation of the Moors and their Islamic culture; even after their departure, the architecture of the region remained forever influenced.

Finally, the historical development of science must not be forgotten. Only as new discoveries in materials and techniques were made could architecture progress.

■ structural unity

Every design consists of an effort to reconcile a form and its context. It is the context, in association with the architect's stock of experience, that prompts the first ideas. The process develops as the architect uses both personal and general experience to analyse the extent of the problem. These two types of experience are very different: personal experience is predominantly direct and subjective, while general experience consists of a variety of indirect material gathered through impersonal sources. The information is like a huge collection of jigsaw pieces; out of this random collection the architect begins to assemble a completely new picture in three dimensions. The "pieces" represent preliminary considerations – including the purpose of the building, its site, the client's resources, and possible materials. The initial steps forward will be hesitant and open-ended, analysing possibilities and detecting alternative relationships, and gradually moving towards creating a new order. The design process must be cyclic, for each new relationship that is exposed will affect and be affected by the others. As the cycle develops, the architect will tend to opt for solutions which further his original intention, and to make choices which best overcome the obstacles which constitute the original problem.

Every building inevitably reflects the force or weakness of the original concept. If the pattern of relationships between all the parts of the design seem complete and self-sufficient, and yet there is only a tenuous link with his original intention, the finished building will be so far removed from what was anticipated that it will be incomprehensible to its users. On the other hand, if the solution does not extend very far beyond basic requirements, it will be too obvious and predictable. To be successful a design must encourage new and unexpected uses as well as having its roots in the original proposal. The tension between these two aspects is what endows a building with a meaning beyond the level which is a mere sum of its parts.

RIGHT Both history and religion are evident influences in the glowing sandstone of this Indian pillar, which both supports and decorates a Muslim interior.

ABOVE All Souls Church, London (1822, Nash). John Nash (1752–1835) was the greatest developer/planner of his time; this simple but effective church was sited at the end of his famous Regent Street (since remodelled).

► vitruvius

Vitruvius was born Marcus Vitruvius Pollio probably sometime half-way through the 1st century BC. A Roman architect and an engineer, it is nevertheless as an author that his name is revered today, for it was through his writings on the subject of architecture – *De architectura* – that the techniques and principles of Classical construction design were first written down. (In fact, Pliny later included some of these writings in his *Natural History*.)

As an architect, Vitruvius is known only to have been responsible for a basilica at Fano (Fanum) on the northern Adriatic coast of Italy. His treatise was based on his own work, however, and on the works of some famous Greek architects of two or more centuries earlier. Dedicated to "the Emperor", *De architectura* is written in an essentially Hellenist style: Vitruvius was rather disappointed in the contemporary Roman styles of architecture and was concerned that the Classical methods of the Greeks should be appreciated and not lost. The work is divided into ten books.

These books contain a wealth of information, sometimes contradictory but nevertheless very detailed, giving an unprecedented insight into Classical building disciplines. Vitruvius describes the principles of symmetry, harmony and proportion, the design of temples, the construction of theatres and information on their siting, foundations and acoustics, the desirability of different materials, the education of the architect and many other relevant topics.

Approximately 50 copies of this work survived through the Middle Ages, although the master-builders of that period seemed to rely on them only for geometric and structural formulas. Not until Italian artists and philosophers in the fourteenth and fifteenth centuries began to analyse Greek and Roman ruins and compare their findings with Vitruvius' theories, was continuity in the development of Western architecture reestablished.

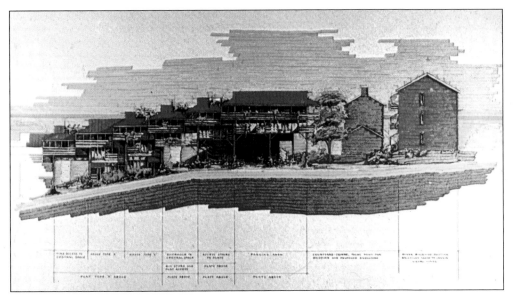

LEFT The coloured elevation is part of a design for a housing scheme by an architectural student. The project was to design a mixed housing development for an actual site. The development had to include bungalows for the elderly, single-person flats and two-, three- and four-bedroom houses.

■ stone

STONE IS THE OLDEST building material known to man. The origins of stone date back to a period nearly 4,000 million years ago. Recorded history is a mere 6,000 years old, so the use of stone by mankind in the ancient structures of Egypt and Greece represents a mere fraction of its life as an inorganic substance.

Over these millions of years, the continually evolving structure of the Earth's crust has produced a wide variety of mineral outcrops. None of these deposits are identical. This great variety of rock, sometimes found in intense proximity as in Britain, has resulted in widely differing specimens, ranging from dense crystalline formations capable of taking a very high polish, to deeply faulted and fissured varieties whose course and variegated mineral structure exposes its own strata.

Due to its crystalline formation, stone is only able to withstand limited forces when used in a mode of tension. For this reason, traditional building development has exploited the material in compression. As with grain in timber, the crystalline formation of most rock has a distinct structure known as the "bed", a name which, as it suggests, describes the relative axis, direction or position of the stone as it originated in the ground, slowly solidifying and hardening over a period of millions of years. With the exception of sedimentary stones which are riven or split much as logs, it has been conventional practice to detail stonework so that individual pieces are exposed with the bed lying in the same direction as it did when the stone was in the ground. No two blocks of stone are alike, a quality of the material which stonemasons have always respected and exploited.

Drilling, blasting, splitting and wedging are all well-tried methods of extraction. Since the beginning of the twentieth century, more efficient production has been achieved in some quarries by the use of continuous wire sawing. Loops of wire up to several hundred yards long are threaded over pulleys from a central motor, descend into the quarry, are threaded around the stone to be cut, and are then pulled

ABOVE A detail from an Ionic capital, this shows stone's incomparable ability to accommodate minute carving or sculpturing in curves and in geometric patterns and for it to withstand erosion.

ABOVE In the Corinthian order, carefully sculptured acanthus leaves emulate the precise shape of the leaves in nature.

ABOVE Granite's stern aspect was used by the Inca people of Peru to build city and fortress walls. The dry joints fit together exactly.

back up again to the source of power. More recently, various methods of heat-processing, such as thermal lances and flame-finishing, have become common practice.

In the simplest form of stone building, stones lying on the ground were gathered up and piled one on top of the other in a decreasing silhouette to form cones, cairns and walls. Although the methods by which the more massive blocks of stone were quarried and transported is largely a mystery, much speculation also surrounds their extraction from the rock. Equal speculation surrounds the method by which the stones were raised into the vertical position and how the horizontal members were then positioned on top. The most credible theory is that earth banks were built up and then hollowed out, so that the vertical members could be lowered into the pits formed in this way. Once the vertical members were positioned, the horizontal members would be rolled and dragged up the false earth embankment to take their place on top of their partners.

Within this family of early structures are the megalithic, Neolithic gallery graves – long narrow chambers – of 3000–1800 B.C. found in France, some of the first examples of stone arcading enclosing interior space to be found in Europe. It is interesting to compare these structures, and that of Stonehenge, with those being built in Egypt at the same time. At the other extreme, craftsmen have worked the rock-face in situ, as Petra in Jordan in A.D. 120.

The great majority of stone structures have been built from pieces of stone designed to be bedded together to form a continuous fabric – an early form of prefabrication. By working and tooling the profile, the particular stone is either designed to be read as a homogeneous surface, such as the fluid, continuous structures of late Gothic arcades, or as a series of separate vertical and horizontal components, such as the framed construction of the Parthenon, or the block-on-block formation of the Florentine palazzos of the fifteenth century. In arcades, the nearly horizontal force of the roof is visually reconciled as being integral and continuous with the vertical shafts.

The main stream of architectural development in stone has been based upon organized systems of assembly. Examples such as those mentioned previously have relied upon premeditated projection of the structure, which has determined the size and proportion of each piece of stone before it has been won from the raw rock. The examples to be examined here rely largely on repetitive components arranged to form a continuous arcaded enclosure. This method of construction originated in a "post-and-lintel", or columnar-and-trabeated, arrangement of horizontal and vertical components. The horizontal members carried the roof loads which were supported in turn by the vertical members.

As experience of the nature of the material grew, so did an understanding of the engineering principles of what has become known as the science of statics and dynamics. The advantages of building in stone by establishing hierarchies of space also emerged, resulting from the complex, three-dimensional geometry which is appropriate for the exploitation of stone in compression. This understanding reached two great apogees in the history of stone building: the ancient, Classical Greek temples of the fifth century B.C. and the Gothic cathedrals of northern Europe, built between the tenth and fourteenth centuries. It was in this latter period that horizontal roof members and vertical column members became tooled, worked and profiled into a continuous, almost plastic composition of ribs and shafts. At the same time, despite the fluency, a clear representation of the structural anatomy can easily be understood. All subsequent architectural developments have been in the shadow of these two important ages of architectural refinement.

It is possible to trace an increasing sophistication and awareness, as stone became refined and lightened in a conscious attempt to "dematerialize" stonework, a process that resulted in the high Gothic of northern Europe. Nowadays, it is frequently used as a respectable veneer in institutional public building or organizations anxious to project a picture of well-established importance.

ABOVE Athenian Treasury, Delphi, Greece (490 B.C.). An exquisite small building in the lower part of the town. This early Doric structure was the first to be built entirely out of marble.

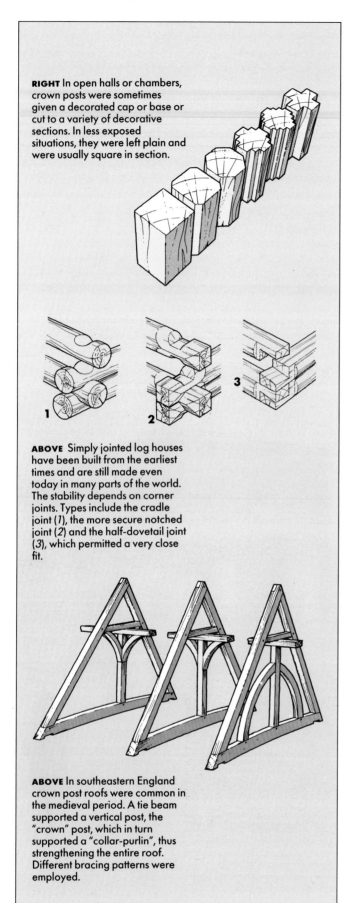

RIGHT In open halls or chambers, crown posts were sometimes given a decorated cap or base or cut to a variety of decorative sections. In less exposed situations, they were left plain and were usually square in section.

ABOVE Simply jointed log houses have been built from the earliest times and are still made even today in many parts of the world. The stability depends on corner joints. Types include the cradle joint (*1*), the more secure notched joint (*2*) and the half-dovetail joint (*3*), which permitted a very close fit.

ABOVE In southeastern England crown post roofs were common in the medieval period. A tie beam supported a vertical post, the "crown" post, which in turn supported a "collar-purlin", thus strengthening the entire roof. Different bracing patterns were employed.

■ timber

Timber from broad leaf or deciduous trees is called "hardwood", while conifers produce "softwood". Although it is true that hardwoods are generally harder than softwoods, there are exceptions to this rule.

Wood, like all plant material, is cellular and the disposition of these cells produces the characteristic "grain" or pattern on the cut surfaces. Knots are a familiar feature of much timber, and are produced by the embedding of a portion of a branch. The term "conversion" is used to mean the cutting up of a log into sawn timber. The method used has a bearing upon the resultant grain pattern.

Seasoning is the process of drying the natural moisture out of the timber, so that it will relate properly to the humidity condition of its ultimate use without shrinking or warping. It is achieved by air-seasoning naturally in some form of open-sided structure, or by artificially drying in an oven or kiln. Modern kilns are so designed that an accurate control of moisture is achieved.

It is not possible to compile a straightforward chronological list of building techniques, nor is it easy to trace the development of styles throughout the forest areas, since the methods varied with the type and availability of suitable timber. The main historical methods are as follows:
Solid timber construction This method involves building with logs set close together and is found generally in eastern Europe where the vast forests could support the extravagance. It is sometimes referred to as "blockwork" and the method has continued to the present day in Russia, Finland and the alpine areas. This "log-cabin" technique involves horizontal members interlocked at corners by a variety of jointing methods. Shapes are achieved by a progressive lengthening or shortening of the logs.
Half-timber construction This is a framework of structural timber (usually hardwood) infilled with lathing or other materials. It was almost always prefabricated and assembled in sections on the ground, giving rise to the various forms of carpenter's marks found on framed structures. Historically, it attained its greatest sophistication in the northern countries of western Europe and subsequently developed in North America and Scandinavia to become the "balloon" or "platform" framing.
Mast or stave work is a particular style apparent in the churches of Norway, which has little evolutionary connection with solid or half-timber construction.
The post-and-beam or "trabeated" style found its best expression in China and Japan, having travelled with Buddhism from India. This method shares with mast work the principle of entirely non-load-bearing walls.

Modern timber-framed structures are assembled from standardized softwood components. In turn, these rely on the careful selection of material which has been graded for stress, according to its particular use within the finished building.

The four basic methods of contemporary timber building are as follows.

Stick construction is used mainly in North America, Scandinavia and Japan. Precut timber elements are delivered to the site and assembled. In Britain, individual builders with small sites use this method, as do self-build groups. One of the great exponents of this method is the architect Walter Segal who, over the last 20 years, has been one of the most enthusiastic protagonists of timber-framed housing. Segal has come to terms with the increasing strictures of building control and regulations and produced a series of delightfully designed houses with a Japanese flavour, which celebrate the authentic use of timber and achieve economy by simple, efficient structure and detail.

Balloon frame construction In this method, the external wall panels are fabricated in various widths, but extend to two storeys in height and are therefore erected in one operation, so that the intermediate floors are suspended from the full height studs. The size of the panels restricts flexibility and manoeuvrability.

Platform frame construction This is the predominant method of timber-frame construction in Britain. Wall panels are fabricated (usually in the factory) in storey heights and floors are then constructed on top of ground floor wall panels, acting as a permanent base for the upper wall panels.

The panels are of a size which can be easily placed into position. The flexibility of this method allows freedom of design with effective and speedy construction.

Many English new towns have recently used this method of construction for their large low-rise housing programmes. Basildon, Milton Keynes, Northampton, Peterborough, Warrington and the Midland Housing Consortium have all built schemes of this type.

Volumetric construction This method entails the fabrication of entire buildings or parts of buildings in the factory and their subsequent transportation, in a virtually finished state, to the site for erection on prepared foundations. Normal preparation includes sanitary fittings, pre-plumbing, wiring and decoration. This type of construction can ensure rapid provision of very cheap houses, but the economic necessity for rigorous standardization, together with limitations on size of units for transportation can constrict the architect a great deal.

Timber is an essential component of buildings constructed in all other materials – generally, as scaffolding or levers, or, specifically, as centering for masonry, form work and lining for concrete, or fixings for steelwork. Its historical role in the construction of roofs (including stone vaults and domes) is unique, while in the past it has been extensively used as piles for foundations on unstable ground.

Most everyday buildings built in other materials could be copied entirely in timber, but the opposite is certainly not true. The chief reason for this is that the fibrous nature of wood, combined with the use of shaped and pegged joints, enable it to accommodate both linear and rotational tension in structures.

LEFT Little Moreton Hall, Cheshire (1550–59). Historically, there have been three types of ways in which a window is related to structure: as a hole in a masonry wall; as glass filling in a cage of structure; or as an integral part of the structure, where the window and the wall are the same element. Medieval timber buildings showed a unity between the main structure and the windows – both elements were suffused into one decorative and functional whole.

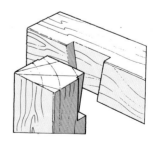

ABOVE The lap dovetail joint is fundamental to British timber building, and was used in most buildings from the thirteenth to the nineteenth centuries.

■ brick

Brick was the first building material to be made by man. It has been used consistently since the Egyptians made bricks of sun-dried mud and straw and the Babylonians discovered the technique of making bricks by burning clay.

There are many practical and economic reasons why the use of brick should have survived: brick is a reasonably priced, standardized product made from an accessible raw material; it performs predictably; it is durable and has good insulating qualities. However, a more important reason for its continuing popularity lies in the close relationship between man and the material. There is a deep satisfaction in constructing buildings from units scaled to a man's hand. The size of the unit orders the building, making it comprehensible, and the unit itself is controlled at all stages of production and use by the skills of the brickmaker and bricklayer. Modern techniques of manufacture and construction now place less emphasis on traditional craft skills, but popular imagination has invested brick with a set of qualities derived from those human activities, and promoted its domestic appeal.

Historically, the use of brick has been influenced by the availability of raw materials. Brickwork traditions have developed in river valleys and alluvial plains which are both rich in clay deposits and lack supplies of building stone. Egypt and Mesopotamia have some of the earliest examples of brickwork; the Romans were quick to see its potential and organized production where they found the raw materials; the European development of the material was carried on in the Netherlands and north Germany around the rivers Oder and Elbe. In England, the art of brickmaking came and went with the Romans, but it revived in the Middle Ages, and since then there has been a steady growth which was accelerated by the Industrial Revolution. Apart from native brick traditions in the Americas, other settlers took brickmaking skills with them. Bricks feature in

many colonial buildings, although brick has never enjoyed the same widespread use in North America as timber.

The basic principles of brickmaking have never changed. It has always been necessary to win the clay from the ground, and then for it to be prepared, shaped, dried and fired. Originally, the manufacture of bricks was carried out as near to the building site as possible – inevitably a time-consuming and labour-intensive process, whose success was governed by the quality of the raw material and the skill of the brickmaker. Developments in machinery in the mid-nineteenth century meant that production was concentrated in the brickfield, and the finished product was distributed by road, rail and canal.

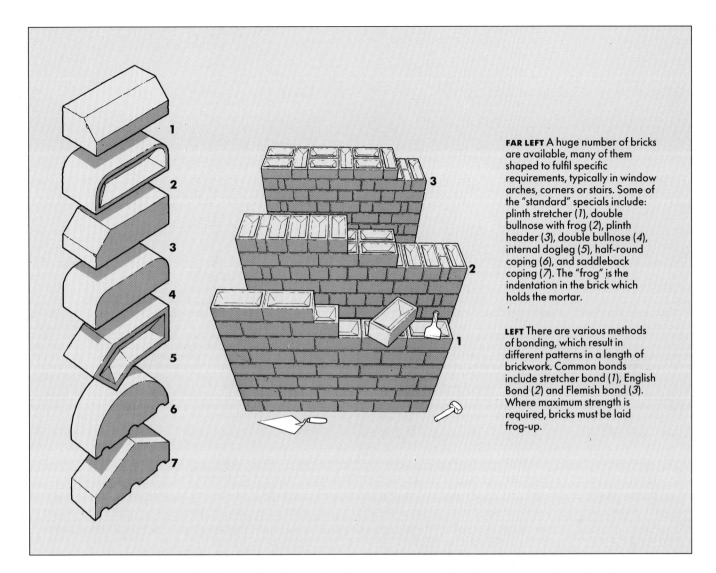

A brick is strong in compression but weak in shear – hard to crush but easy to snap – hence, it is well suited to being part of a load-bearing system where the loads are compressive. Brickwork, although it is an aggregation of small units, relies on mass and the uniform transfer of load. The mass of the material is made up by bedding the bricks in mortar and bonding them together, so that loads are distributed over a larger area through a greater number of bricks. This is in direct contrast to a column-and-beam system of building, where the loads are transferred from the horizontal to the vertical.

Although brickwork as a structural material essentially takes the form of massive solid walls with no openings, it did not take builders long to discover the arch, a technique of forming openings in brick walls by using bricks themselves. It is necessary to support an arch during construction – usually on a timber framework, called centering – but once the arch is complete the centering is removed and the arch stands, always assuming that the work has been properly carried out, and there is sufficient restraint to prevent it spreading. It is a short step from the idea of the arch to the idea of the barrel vault, and builders were eventually able to pierce walls and enclose space between them using a single material. Corbelling – the technique whereby successive courses break forward of the wall face – is another way of enclosing space, especially suitable when the building plan is circular.

Although brickwork is a structural material, it is sometimes used non-structurally, as a panel in a vaulted ceiling or enclosing a steel or reinforced concrete frame building. Brickwork is well suited for this role. Not only is it attractive and durable but also it is possible to cut and shape bricks to fit into irregular spaces.

The bricklayer's skill is the final factor which determines the appearance of brickwork. Apart from the basic requirements of keeping work vertical, maintaining a proper gauge and a correct bond and obtaining the proper horizontal line of each course, there are numerous small adjustments which can be made to brickwork as the work proceeds, because few bricks are precisely the same size and there is nearly always a variation in colour or texture. The good bricklayer will accommodate the differences and the finished work will have a conviction that is easy to recognize but difficult to describe.

ABOVE Ironbridge, Shropshire, England (1779–81). Abraham Darby III (1750–91). Now a pedestrian bridge, this 59m (196ft) semicircular bridge was the first iron bridge in the world. It spans the Severn Gorge and was built with iron smelted at nearby Coalbrookdale, the virtual birthplace of the Industrial Revolution.

■ iron

Iron is the second most common metal and the fourth most common of the elements that make up the earth. Although iron is an element, in commercial usage small quantities of other materials are always present. It is the varying amount of these other elements, principally carbon, that gives us cast-iron, wrought-iron or steel. Cast-iron is the most resistant to corrosion and the easiest to make, so its major use in building predates steel; wrought-iron is the easiest to work; steel is the strongest, but unfortunately the quickest to corrode.

As building materials, iron and steel were very different from the materials that builders had used before. Earlier changes, such as the introduction of brick in late medieval England, had not implied a new architecture, as they could be used for load-bearing walls in much the same way as the stone buildings that they superseded. But iron and steel are much stronger and more expensive than older materials, and so it became logical to use them as linear members, first as tie bars, then as columns and finally as complete frames, with cheaper, more durable materials used to form the walls and to keep the weather out. The history of iron and steel in architecture is, therefore, largely the story of the framed building and how to clothe it comfortably and beautifully, while still acknowledging that powerful frame inside.

Iron is made from iron ore in a blast furnace, and the process is called smelting. In a modern blast furnace, hot air is blown into a mixture of ore, coke and limestone, in a continuous operation, to give a temperature of 2370°F (1300°C). It is a structure of some size and drama, about 260 feet (80 m) high, made of steel with a fireclay lining. The products of smelting are pig iron or cast-iron, hot gases, and slag, which is either thrown away, used for ballast for railway tracks or used in cement manufacture.

Iron is more difficult to smelt than copper, and consequently the Iron Age came after the Bronze Age. The first iron used was probably meteoric iron, which needed no smelting. When the Europeans first went to the American continent they found that the Aztecs had no knowledge of smelting, but used meteoric iron which they regarded as more precious than gold.

The first smelting of iron probably took place in Asia around 2000 B.C. Its use subsequently spread to the Mediterranean countries. Iron was in general use in the Classical world for making tools and weapons, but not for building.

In medieval times, the iron industry grew, and the advent of the cannon made the ironmasters crucial men in any nation. The iron was smelted by the use of charcoal, and England's forests were cleared to provide this material. In the later eighteenth century, Abraham Darby (1711–63) at Coalbrookdale began smelting with coke instead of charcoal, and, as a result, the quality of iron increased dramatically and the price dropped. Darby needed a bigger market for his iron than cannon, and turned to building and engineering structures.

During the early nineteenth century, William Fairbairn (1789–1874) and Eaton Hodgkinson (1798–1861) applied the mathematical studies that had been undertaken in France to the iron structures under way in England and produced systems for analysing and calculating the forces within a structure. The engineer with his slide rule began to take over from the craftsman when it came to making decisions – just in time for the construction of new bridges to take the heavy loads of the railways.

The experiments of Hodgkinson and Fairbairn revealed the limitations of cast-iron for structural work. For a while, reliance was placed on wrought-iron, and, in 1850, the Cooper Union Building in New York City was built with a structure of rolled wrought-iron beams. However, a series of bridge failures, notably the disasters at Ashtabula, Ohio (1876) and Firth of Tay, Scotland (1879), resulted in a generation of engineers who looked increasingly to steel as the better structural material.

Iron was traditionally used cast in moulds of oil-bound sand, but steel can be finished in many ways. Like iron, it can be cast; it can be drawn into thin wires or rolled into thin sheets which can be strengthened by corrugations. The most characteristic steel form in building is the rolled section, where steel ingots are rolled to standard profiles – I-beams, channels, tees and hollow sections. These have the advantages of being structurally efficient, easy to join and standardized, the last being important now that the calculation of dimensions is a codified procedure, enforced and checked by a government inspectorate.

The Iron Bridge at Coalbrookdale (1779) had members which were interlocked and then wedged together. This was an awkward way of joining and did not guarantee that stresses were passed from member to member, so bolting soon became the normal procedure. The introduction of riveting gave a tighter fit than the early bolts, but modern bolts have largely eliminated that advantage. During the First World War, welding came into its own in the munitions industry, and its use spread to shipbuilding, bridgebuilding and the construction industry. It was generally found to be more expensive to weld a joint than to rivet it, but the extra cost was more than offset by the possibility of using lighter members now that they would not be weakened by holes for rivets. Although welding is now the normal method of joining structural steels, there are still problems with welding very heavy sections and with some alloy steels.

For further information on the development of iron and steel, see the historical section of this book.

TOP Pompidou Centre, Paris (Richard Rogers & Renzo Piano, 1971–77). Described by its architects as 'a giant Meccano set', the Pompidou Centre caused a storm of controversy.

ABOVE Grand Magasin du Printemps, Paris (1881–89). The interior cornice and rise of the central dome in an iron-built French department store.

■ concrete

Concrete is a plain and unpretentious material, already some 2,000 years old. Reinforced concrete, on the other hand, has a relatively short history and is quite a different sort of material. Brash and versatile, it has stamped its image all over the modern world. In the twentieth century, reinforced concrete has been used to perpetrate both unspeakable eyesores and structures of great economy, ingenuity and delight.

Of all the major building materials, concrete is the real hybrid. Like the latest group, plastics, it is a composite; unlike plastics, its constituents are to be found in their natural state. In its simplest, mass form, concrete is a cheap and efficient substitute for masonry. (Initially, it was seen as such and the artificial stone label still lingers.) There are only three basic components and all of these are available worldwide: cement, aggregate and water.

The cement, nowadays, is almost invariably a grade of "Portland" – so called because its inventor likened its appearance to Portland stone – composed usually of limestone, silica, aluminous clay and gypsum. Portland is far superior in strength and durability to its predecessor lime cement, and has largely superseded it. High-alumina cement (HAC), which contains bauxite instead of clay, is even stronger.

The aggregate is composed of fine sand and, in most cases, various sizes and shapes of coarse stone or gravel. Lightweight aggregates such as pumice, foamed slag, expanded clay and vermiculite are also used, particularly for precast building blocks. Cellular concrete, lighter still, is obtained with air-entrained bubbles.

The exact nature and proportioning of these ingredients is of vital importance to the performance of the finished product. There is good, bad and indifferent concrete; and the "mix" will vary according to the job that it is called upon to do. (A typical specification for a slab, for example would be written as 1 : 3 : 6 – the respective proportions of cement, fine and coarse aggregate.)

Much development has been concentrated on improving the appearance of "visual" concrete – the type of concrete that is designed to be seen, rather than to be covered up. Attempts to achieve a significant difference in the colour of cement, by the addition of pigments, has not been very successful: time and exposure result in fading. The shades of grey, however, can be brightened by using white cement, silver sand and a near-white granite when making up the concrete. More importantly, the surface texture can be treated in interesting ways. Finishes can be varied by treating the surface directly or by applying different types of aggregate. The marks of shuttering can be left on the surface to give a board-marked finish; profiled and patterned finishes can be created by the use of special linings such as ribbed aluminium. One of the most effective profiled finishes is deep vertical ribbing, which encourages rainwater to run down the recessed grooves. Concrete is also a perfect sculptor's medium. With sufficient skill and dedication, the artist can model entire facades in bold relief, by casting it against carved polystyrene forms.

The essential feature of concrete is that it has great strength in compression, but very little in tension or shear. While it can withstand a massive axial load, it will not hold together under any comparable sort of pull. The modulus of elasticity of concrete is also exceedingly low and inconstant: that is to say, there is a tendency to shift or creep – a not entirely damaging phenomenon, technically known as "plastic flow".

The insertion of steel rods, wire or mesh into the concrete matrix completely transforms the performance of the material. Previous deficiencies in tension and shear are made good, so that the material is capable of spanning. Thanks to the continuity of the steel reinforcement, separate elements of a building become homogeneous and monolithic. In that all the components act together, a reinforced concrete beam-and-slab system is structurally more efficient than, for example, a wooden floor composed of separate joists. When a series of beams and columns are rigidly connected together they form a frame which distributes the loads and stresses of one part to all the others. Effectively, the entire framework becomes a unified whole.

ABOVE Notre Dame, Le Raincy, near Paris (Auguste Perret, 1922–23). With its basilica plan, slender columns and stained-glass windows, this church echoed Gothic architecture, but with one outstanding difference – it was made out of reinforced concrete. The stained glass was designed by Maurice Denis.

LEFT Notre Dame du Haut, Ronchamp, France (Le Corbusier, 1950–55). Conscientious readers of Le Corbusier's writings might be surprised at this late work which seems contrary to his mechanistic theories. Visitors to this pilgrimage church should ignore earlier propaganda and enjoy this amazing piece of sculpture on its own terms. The rough-cast concrete walls have small, scattered windows set in deep embrasures which create a magical sequence of internal illumination programmed by the passage of the sun as it moves around the hill-top site.

BELOW LEFT This monument built in Como in 1936 by Cataneo is an exuberant demonstration of the engineering feats possible with reinforced concrete. Each band of concrete is marked with vertical lines, adding to the illusion.

The proper construction of a reinforced concrete beam, column or slab in situ – that is to say, poured in place on the job – calls for a great deal of care and attention to detail. There are many factors, not forgetting the human element, that will affect the finished product.

The denser the concrete, the stronger it will be. Varying the type and quantity of cement also affects ultimate strength, and especially the rate of hardening. High water content reduces strength and increases shrinkage. There should be no more water than is necessary to achieve the correct chemical reactions and minimum workability.

Design of the shuttering against which the concrete is poured is crucial: it has to be rigid, well supported and without leaking joints. Every surface imperfection will be accurately transmitted to the concrete – for good or bad, depending on the designer and the contractor.

Concrete cannot, in most circumstances, be continuously poured. At the end of the working shift there will be a construction or "day" joint.

Although shuttering can be reused, basically by treating the casting face with a release agent, there are limits to the number of times that a piece of timber, ply or even metal can safely be employed again. Eventually, the shutter must be replaced; throughout its period of use it is necessary to take it down, clean it, and reassemble it in new locations.

The obvious alternative is to pour concrete against a lining which remains an integral part of the building. Virtually any material that is keyed or rough on the unseen side is suitable, provided its coefficient of expansion is not too dissimilar from concrete. Materials most commonly used today include thin elements of precast concrete, woodwool, and glass-reinforced cement (GRC).

Precasting, in common with so many other technical advances, demands standardization and repetition (disciplines which, in themselves, reduce cost and time). Compared with casting on site, there are formidable advantages: industrialized production methods are more efficient; factory conditions improve quality control; the designer is offered a wider range of finishes; the manufactured component is superior in accuracy, strength and weathering; and on-site time is drastically reduced.

However, given the need for continuity in the finished structure, new problems can arise on site with the jointing of the individual components. Structural engineers tend to view the whole construction process as primarily revolving around the connections, for it is these which must transmit stress, take up movement, and exclude weather.

In a structure composed of precast frame elements, continuity across the joints can be achieved by leaving projecting reinforcement and pouring concrete around it, or by bolting where there is least stress. In simple portal frames, for example, these joints will occur at the points where there is no bending moment. Similarly, as may be witnessed by anyone driving along a motorway, the main span of a precast concrete bridge (in all likelihood, prestressed also) is supported, at these points, by open

joggled joints that incorporate rollers, permitting the beams to take up thermal movement.

A great amount of effort has been directed at designing perfect systems of connection – yet contemporary buildings still leak and occasionally collapse.

Though the most interesting developments in precast concrete have taken place in the realm of custom-designed units, it should not be overlooked that a vast industry has grown up for the production of a host of off-the-peg components. These range from basic shed frames for light industrial and agricultural use, through domestic garages, to such humble everyday items as lintels, sills, copings, posts, kerbs, bollards and paving slabs.

Reference should also be made to the universal wall block, which, because of its superior thermal performance and relative cheapness, has largely superseded brick for partitions and the inner face of cavity walls.

In the short history of reinforced concrete there has been no more far-reaching and exciting technical achievement than the successful application of prestressing. Yet again, the underlying principle is simple, clear and far from new.

Mass concrete has negligible tensile strength and placing steel reinforcing bars in the bottom part of a beam, for example, makes good this lack, enabling the beam to span horizontally and to carry superimposed loads. However, where sheer weight of the material and depth of beam is incompatible with the load and span – as occurs in wide-span structures such as bridges – this standard solution becomes unwieldy, uneconomic or even impossible. The reason behind this incompatibility lies in the imperfect interaction of two totally dissimilar materials. If the steel were to be stressed to its full capacity, the surrounding concrete would be in excessive tension.

What happens in a prestressed concrete beam is that the tensioned, extended steel attempts to revert to its original length and, in so doing, compresses the surrounding concrete. When bending takes place under load, the concrete will not be in tension until all the gratuitous compressive stress is used up. In practice, the amount of prestress applied is carefully set so that the concrete is effectively free from tension and the "dead load" or weight of the beam itself has been eliminated. (The downward load has been transmitted to a horizontal one, the stresses being taken up internally in the steel cables.)

The immediate result is that cracking is minimal and controlled, and there is an improvement in elasticity, resilience, structural continuity and weather resistance. Above all, a higher strength to weight ratio means that far longer spans become possible, and with less material. In comparison with conventional reinforced concrete, up to 70 percent concrete and 85 percent steel can be saved. Since, in their stressed condition, the two materials are balanced – and as all the concrete is now contributing – the profile of a prestressed beam begins to resemble a conventional I-section steel joist.

The presenting steel elements, commonly high-tensile wires or cables, can be tensioned in one of two ways:

TOP Yale University, Hockey Rink, Connecticut, USA (Saarinen, 1958). A massive serpentine concrete beam, sculpturally cantilevered and counterbalanced each end, supports cables which carry and mould the cladding to this vast and whale-like roof.

ABOVE TWA Terminal, Kennedy Airport, New York (1962). Saarinen felt that air terminals should reflect something of the excitement of air travel. His theory was superbly translated into this Expressionist building in shell concrete.

LEFT The bold and simple-looking lines of Sydney's Opera House belie the complexity of the concrete construction, which is both innovative and imaginative.

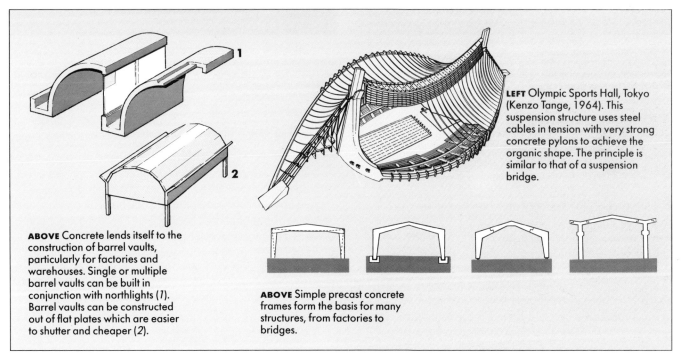

LEFT Olympic Sports Hall, Tokyo (Kenzo Tange, 1964). This suspension structure uses steel cables in tension with very strong concrete pylons to achieve the organic shape. The principle is similar to that of a suspension bridge.

ABOVE Concrete lends itself to the construction of barrel vaults, particularly for factories and warehouses. Single or multiple barrel vaults can be built in conjunction with northlights (1). Barrel vaults can be constructed out of flat plates which are easier to shutter and cheaper (2).

ABOVE Simple precast concrete frames form the basis for many structures, from factories to bridges.

before the concrete is poured, or after the concrete has hardened. Prestressing is by no means confined to horizontal beams. It can be equally applied to lattice girders and trusses, to cylindrical forms such as silos, to dams, and to vertical masts and tower structures.

Ferro-cemento is the name coined by its inventor, Pier Luigi Nervi (b.1891), for thin slabs of cement reinforced with steel mesh. Precast off plaster moulds, ferro-cemento was used for moveable shuttering, permanent formwork, and

for structural units. The finished surface was extremely smooth, needing no additional treatment or maintenance.

Gunite is the application of concrete pneumatically sprayed onto steel mesh or an "inflatable". The apparently solid and very thick front wall of Le Corbusier's Chapel of Notre Dame, Ronchamp (1955) is, in fact, faced with a gunite skin. Sprayed concrete combines well with steel cable suspension nets, and its special properties include high strength and density.

ABOVE John Hancock Tower, Boston, Massachusetts (1969–73, IM Pei). Reflecting glass enforces a feeling of separation from the surrounding world and emphasizes the soaring simplicity of this building.

ABOVE Maison de Verre, Paris (1931, Pierre Chareau). In Japanese houses, the use of carefully proportioned translucent paper panels gives a lightness and delicacy to the interiors that many modern architects have sought to emulate. When the Japanese influence was at its height in the first decades of the twentieth century, European architects used glass blocks to produce gridded translucent interiors.

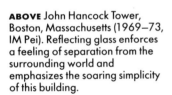

glass

The discovery that the three common materials – sand, soda and lime – could be fused together by heat to form a hard transparent material is generally thought to have originated in the Middle East, sometime before 1500 B.C. Glass was at first used only for decoration, but when it was realized that in its molten state it could be cast or blown into shapes, simple hollow vessels were also produced.

The Romans did much to perfect these techniques and were even able to make a type of flat glass for use in buildings by rolling out the hot glass onto a hard flat table. The surface of this glass was rough and it was not very transparent. Modern sheet glass techniques date from developments made late in the nineteenth century, in the United States. The basic glass mix or "frit" consists of 15 parts sand (silica), five parts soda, and four parts limestone, to which up to one-third as much again of scrap glass or "cullet" is added, to assist the melting. The function of the limestone is to harden the glass. The soda or soda ash (sodium carbonate or bicarbonate) is added to help make the silica melt at a lower temperature.

The glass mix is fed into a tank and after it has been melted at a temperature of around 2700°F (1500°C), it is drawn up out of the tank on a bar of glass called the "bait". As soon as the glass has cooled enough and the surface is sufficiently hard not to be marked, it is passed between pairs of rollers which pull the glass and flatten it to the required thickness. At this stage, the rollers can be patterned to give decorative or obscured glass. The glass, whether patterned or plain, is then drawn up through a cooling tower or "lehr", and cut off in sheets.

The surface finish of glass produced by this method is smooth and has a natural brilliance, without the need for grinding and polishing. However, the drawing process does impart strains on the glass which show as distortions. Such glass cannot be used where great clarity is required and although the process is inexpensive, and is commonly used in horticulture and domestic applications, it is gradually being replaced in general use by float glass. *Crown glass* This method was widely used in the Middle Ages. Glass was formed into the shape of a small pear by blowing, heating and rolling on a polished metal surface, until it formed a sphere. This sphere was broken off from the blowpipe and its base was sealed on to an iron rod or "punty", and the whole was reheated and spun, the centrifugal force pulling the glass out into a flat circular plate up to about 5 feet (1.5m) in diameter. As the glass did not touch another surface in its malleable state, the surface had a high polish and lustrous appearance. On the other hand, only small panes could be cut from the circle and both the "crown" or bull's eye in the centre and the outer parts were usually wasted. The process was widely used until the nineteenth century, when it was replaced by improved versions of cylinder glass.

Cylinder glass This process involves blowing hot glass into a cylinder shape which is then slit along its length, opened out, flattened and cut to size. Up until the end of the seventeenth century, it produced both ordinary window glass and, after grinding and polishing, plate glass, but the process could only produce lengths of 4 feet (1.3m) or so, before the glass became too thin to polish.

In the eighteenth century, improved techniques made it possible to produce larger panes. The cylinder was allowed to cool before being slit from end to end with an iron or diamond, then it was reheated just sufficiently to open it out on to a flat piece of polished glass. This gave an acceptable finish to the glass surface, without the need for subsequent polishing. Although the larger cylinder resulted in larger panes, the transparency of window glass produced by this method was still marred.

Plate glass In the seventeenth century, the French made large "plates" of glass by pouring liquid glass onto a metal table and rolling it flat. The table and roller gave the glass a rough finish which had to be made smooth by grinding and polishing, first with sand and water, then with felt pads charged with rouge.

The term "plate" glass derives from its original use in the sevententh and eighteenth centuries as coach glass or mirror glass – the silvered glass being known as "looking-glass plates."

In the 1920s, a method was devised for pouring a continuous ribbon of glass. With continuous grinding and polishing, this improved the speed at which plate glass could be made. However, this remains an expensive process and is gradually being superseded by float glass.

Float glass This process was introduced in England in 1959. It consists of a continuous ribbon of molten glass up to 11 feet (3.3m) wide, which is poured out of a melting furnace, to float along the surface of a bath of molten tin. The ribbon is held in a chemically controlled atmosphere at a high temperature to melt out the impurities. The ribbon is gradually cooled on the tin so that the surfaces are hard enough not to be marked by the rollers in the annealing lehr. The glass produced by this method has a uniform thickness which can be varied to suit particular requirements and has a bright, fine polished surface.

The process was further modified in 1967 to allow metallic ions to be driven into the glass as it passes through the float bath. This produces the bronze-tinted glasses so widely used in modern buildings.

Laminated glass This is a safety glass made by sandwiching a thin layer of transparent plastic between two sheets of glass. It was orginally developed for car windows because when the glass breaks, the pieces are held safely in place by the plastic. Today, the middle layer is usually a vinyl plastic. A combination of toughened and laminated glass in multiple layers produces bullet-proof glass.

Wired glass A wire mesh fed in between the rollers when the glass is made gives the glass the tensile strength that brittle glass lacks. The combination is tough and is extensively used in rooflights or as a fire barrier, where the heat would expand and shatter other types of glass.

TOP During the daytime, reflective glass when seen from below can make a building seem to dissolve and form part of the skyscape. In other conditions such buildings can look monolithic.

ABOVE Johnson House, New Canaan, Connecticut, USA (1949). Philip Johnson (b1906). Although clearly inspired by Mies, Johnson created for himself an individual masterpiece in the genre of steel and glass.

■ plastics

Plastic is not just the newest of the primary construction materials available to the building designer today, it is also the most challenging. The basic building materials – brick, stone and timber – are natural raw materials with a history as long as man. Even metal, glass and concrete are processed from natural materials and their basic principles have been understood from ancient times. Plastic has no such pedigree. There is no deep wealth of experience in its use, nor is it yet associated with any clear cultural meaning. It is unique in being an entirely manmade material, a product essentially of the twentieth century.

It is not surprising that when plastics became available, their introduction followed the time-honoured route of development of all new materials. The first applications of plastics were supplementary to traditional materials, providing better paints for wood, protective coatings for metals, insulants for brick and concrete, damp-proof membranes for roofs, sealants for stone, and so on. However, as industrialization tempted skilled craftsmen away from the construction site to the better conditions and pay in the factories, labour costs began to rise and hence, the cost of traditional materials rose as well, since the production of these were labour-intensive. This development coincided, in the 1950s and 1960s, with a massive increase in building output and a higher standard of living, which led to a demand for faster, cheaper construction with better thermal performance and lesser maintenance. As the properties of plastics became better

known, they developed from being supplements to traditional materials, to actual replacements for them.

There are two basic categories of plastics, distinguished by their behaviour when heated. The first category, "thermosetting" plastics, become soft when heated and can be shaped, but upon further heating, they become stiff and solid and cannot then be softened again.

The second category, called simply "thermoplastics", soften when heated and become stiff and solid again when cooled. Unlike the thermosets, by further heating and cooling these states can be repeated. Generally, whereas both plastics remain sensitive to variations in temperature, the thermosets are less so, have better resistance to stress, better fire endurance, and can be made more rigid, while the thermoplastics can be processed into more complex shapes. Both types of plastics have many different applications in building.

The chemistry of plastics hinges upon the element carbon, and its exceptional ability to form compounds with other elements particularly with one or more of the five elements hydrogen, oxygen, nitrogen, chlorine and fluorine. Every element consists of small particles, or atoms, unique to that element. To form compounds, the atoms of the elements involved must combine and the resultant combination of atoms is called a molecule. Most molecules consist of only a very few atoms. Water, for instance, has just three, two of hydrogen and one of oxygen (H_2O). Plastic molecules, however, can consist of many thousands of atoms, and it is the size and shape of these molecules that differentiate plastic compounds from others.

RIGHT Water Research Centre, Swindon (Architects Design Partnership). The use of plastics in this building illustrates the variety of appliations of the material in construction. Neoprene gaskets seal the glazing on the front elevation; pastic-based paints cover the external steelwork; and complex profiled GRP panels are used for cladding.

To make these large molecules, chemists start from quite simple molecular structures called monomers. Ethylene is a monomer, having just six atoms, two of carbon and four of hydrogen. By linking these simple structures together into a pattern, a more complex molecular combination can be formed called a polymer. The process is called polymerization. When the basic ethylene molecule is polymerized so that it has 4,000 carbon atoms and 8,000 hydrogen atoms, the resultant polymer is a plastic material, polyethylene or polythene.

The polymerization process results in a variety of forms of raw plastic – in basic forms such as powders, granules and liquids or in semi-finished forms, such as sheets, films, foams, rods or tubes. A number of different shaping techniques are needed to make these into articles and these techniques have a strong influence on the use to which the plastic can be put and the shape of the final product. These different shaping techniques are also already beginning to change the appearance of buildings.

Plastics such as acrylic can be simply formed into sheets by heating the raw material with a catalyst to form a viscous liquid. When this is poured between two polished surfaces, such as glass, and allowed to cool, it will harden to a sheet of even thickness with a smooth, flat surface. Transparent acrylic sheets made in this way are widely used as an alternative to glass.

Flexible films and sheets can be made in two ways. PVC sheet is made by mixing the raw plastic with plasticizers, pigments and stabilizers, then heating it to about 340°F (170°C) and drawing it through a row of hot rollers. The continuous sheet of thin molten plastic which results is cooled; it then solidifies and can be trimmed.

Polythene, on the other hand, is made into a thin sheet by drawing out molten plastic into a tube. Cold air is blown into the tube to make it into a thin continuous balloon-like film which is solidified by cooling and then flattened and wound on to rollers. By cutting one side of the tube along its length, it can be opened out to form a flat sheet.

To make drawn shapes or extrusions in plastic, thermoplastic powder or granules are fed from a hopper into a heated barrel. Inside the barrel, a rotating screw forces the softened plastic out through a die which is shaped to give the required cross-section. Dies can be made to produce flat sheets, rods, bars or planks, both hollow and solid, and even coating for wire or other materials. The material which results has a uniform profile and thickness which cannot be varied along its length, but the length itself is limited only by the ability to handle it conveniently.

The larger plastics components used in building, such as wall and roof panels, are more commonly moulded from the rigid thermosetting resins. Polyester resin together with glass fibre reinforcements produces a material known better as glass reinforced plastic (GRP), or fibreglass.

THERMOPLASTICS	USES
POLYETHYLENE (POLYTHENE)	packaging components – films for greenhouse covers and inflatable structures – insulation for outdoor cables – piping – ropes – metal coatings – swimming pool linings
POLYPROPYLENE	chairs – baths and sinks – piping – ropes – ironmongery
POLYVINYL CHLORIDE (PVC)	floor finishes – suspended ceilings – rooflights – damp-proof membranes – metal coatings – chair covers – cable insulation – shower curtains – piping – foamed for window frames and furniture components – inflatable structures – pool linings – panel facings – weather-proofing seals – skirtings
POLYSTYRENE (INCLUDING ABS – ACRYLONITRILE BUTADIENE STYRENE)	expanded for insulation and as lightweight concrete aggregate – shutter linings – foamed for window frames and furniture components – suspended ceilings – ironmongery – covings
POLYMETHYL METHACRYLATE (ACRYLIC, e.g. "PERSPEX")	glazing – baths, sinks and shower cabinets – furniture – fascia panels – suspended ceilings
POLYCARBONATE	glazing – furniture – household goods
POLYVINYL ACETATE	emulsion paints – adhesives – floor fiinishes – admixtures for mortars and fillers
NYLON (POLYAMIDES)	door furniture – curtain rails – fabrics – ropes
POLYTETRA-FLUORETHYLENE (PTFE e.g. "TEFLON")	coatings to kitchen utensils and roofing fabrics
PHENOL FORMALDEHYDE RESINS (e.g. "BAKELITE")	phenolic paper honeycomb covers to sandwich panels and shells – with tung oil for sealing cork, wood and linoleum – with melamine in decorative laminate panels – glues for plywoods – fuse blocks and meter housings – telephone handsets – saucepan handles – knobs – drawer pulls – desk equipment
UREA FORMALDEHYDE (e.g. "BEETLE")	foamed for cavity insulation – glues for plywood – electric plugs – tableware – lighting reflectors – floor sealers – for waterproofing papers
MELAMINE FORMALDEHYDE (MELAMINE)	decorative laminates – electric plugs – tableware – cladding panel facings
POLYESTER RESINS	with glass fibre to form fibreglass (GRP) – ropes – admixtures for mortars and fillers – floor finishes
EPOXY RESINS (e.g. "ARALDITE")	structural adhesives – metal coatings – admixtures for mortars, fillers and renders
POLYURETHANE	foamed for insulation, sealing strips, cushion and mattress linings – underlays and as core material for sandwich panels – paints – varnishes
POLYORGANO-SILICONE (SILICONE)	cushioning and caulking – weatherproof seals – waterproofing films – polishes, paints, varnishes

■ the ancient egyptians

EGYPTIAN CIVILIZATION PROSPSERED from about 3000 B.C. until its gradual amalgamation into the Greek and then the Roman Empires. Until A.D. 100, Egyptian architecture was highly sophisticated but static – an architecture of monuments. The ruling kings, the Pharaohs, were regarded as god-kings: after death they spent unspecified years in a kind of purgatory, during which their souls inhabited other creatures, to return eventually as fully fledged divinities. To aid this happy metamorphosis, preparations in the form of funeral furnishings were provided in their tombs, which were concealed in the depths of colossal stone monuments, of which the Pyramids are the most familiar. Egyptian temples, unlike those of Greece or the later Christian churches, were entirely exclusive, designed for the god-king only and his or her high priests.

Although Egyptian civilization rose and subsided over a period of 3,000 years, it was comparatively early in its development that the dynastic art and technology of building in stone became consolidated. There was an intense period of early development, followed by 2,000 years of repetitious and eclectic building construction.

The Egyptians used stone in two quite different ways. Firstly, external walls and pylons were detailed to describe a single homogeneous surface upon which were inscribed figures and symbols. Like vast billboards, the calm surface of the background was then exploited by the carving that was subsequently inscribed upon it.

Secondly, the Egyptians will always be known for the construction of their temples and palaces – the first buildings to use post-and-lintel construction. This column and beam system was limited to the interior.

The character of Egyptian architecture stemmed directly from the geological and climatic circumstances of the Nile Valley. The stone was quarried directly from the banks of the Nile, adjacent to the centres of population. The details of the column reaching upwards to make a comfortable connection between the column, and the largely undecorated lintel members, were inspired by the lotus, the papyrus and the palm which were found growing beside the river.

Not fully appreciating the structural potential of stone, Egyptian builders placed columns at relatively close centres to avoid long-span lintel stones at roof level. The columns themselves were also relatively squat in proportion. The pillared (hypostyle) hall at Karnak (1500 B.C.), gives the

impression that the galleries were literally quarried from solid rock.

Although the Pyramids remained the highest buildings in the world for 5,000 years and required methodical ingenuity in construction, by comparison with the temples and palaces higher up the Nile at Luxor, Karnak and Edfu, they remain monuments to engineering rather than architecture. The mathematical accuracy of these constructions is staggering: the four sides of the great pyramid at Giza (c2600–2500 B.C.) are equal to within fractions of a centimetre and the angle of approximately 52° was maintained in the building up, one on another, of some two million blocks of stone, each having been floated down the Nile from Upper Egypt.

BELOW The Great Temple of Ammon, Karnak, Egypt (c1312–1301 B.C.). This temple complex was not built to a single masterplan. It owes its existence to the work of many kings, having started as a modest shrine and only slowly expanding in size and complexity over the centuries. Each individual addition, however, remains in style, so preserving Karnak's architectural integrity as an organic whole. One of the chief features of the complex are the solid stonework pylons on the exteriors and the use of very closely centred columns in the interiors.

The effect is extremely atmospheric and imposing (**INSET CENTRE**). The walls, column shafts and architraves (**INSET RIGHT**) are elaborately decorated with coloured inscriptions and reliefs. As well as lists of kings and tributes to the gods, these decorations include a description of Thutmose III's victory at Megiddo, the earliest known account of a battle.

■ stonehenge

The massive stones that make up the extraordinary monument of Stonehenge near Amesbury in Wiltshire were collected and arranged over the course of some 1,400 years between 2750 and 1300 B.C. There were altogether around 150 stones, some brought from quarries in Wales, some 22 feet (6.7m) high, and some weighing about 45 tonnes. The exact purpose of the careful arrangement of the stones in the various interconnecting circles remains unclear. However, a number of astronomical parallaxes relating to both solar and lunar calendars have been established on a historical basis. It is possible that such astronomical events formed the focus of religious ceremonials.

■ sumeria

The essence of brick building lies in the construction of massive walls, with openings formed by arches and the space between these enclosed by vaults. Evidence of early buildings which fit this description has been found in the alluvial plains of the Tigris and Euphrates. Timber and stone were rare in Mesopotamia; the only material available in abundance was clay. The Babylonians made both sun-dried and kiln-burnt bricks. The former were generally used for the core of the walls, the latter for facing them.

The city of Babylon must have been a remarkable place. Planned on a formal grid with streets parallel to and at

ABOVE Stonehenge, Wiltshire, England (2750–1300 B.C.). An intriguing monument to the ancient world. The axis was aligned with the rising sun on the longest day of the year in the northern hemisphere (21st June).

right-angles with the Euphrates River, the entire city was enclosed by great, thick walls. Inside the walls were terraced towers, large temples and the Palace of Nebuchadnezzar (died 562 B.C.), all built from mud bricks.

The Assyrians conquered Babylon in 1275 B.C. and the Palace of Sargon at Khorsabad (722–705 B.C.) is a good example of the way in which they accepted the limitations imposed by the use of a single material. The Palace was set 50 feet (15m) above the plain on a platform of sun-dried bricks. The building, which covered nearly 25 acres (10 hectares), was planned in three sections: the Seraglio (the formal palace), the Harem (the private rooms) and the Khan (the service rooms), all of which related to a central court 2½ acres (1 hectare) in area. The massive walls, 28 feet (8.5m) thick, and the succession of long narrow spaces grouped around open courtyards give the impression that the building was hollowed out of a huge clay pile.

Bas-reliefs have been found which suggest the Assyrians knew about the construction of domes. Sir Banister Fletcher, in *A History of Architecture*, discerns a link between Assyrian and Byzantine buildings through the work of the Sassanian Dynasty (A.D. 226–642) established near Babylon. The Palace at Sarvistan near Persepolis (A.D. 350) has a triple-arched portico, behind which is a square hall roofed by a brick-built beehive dome.

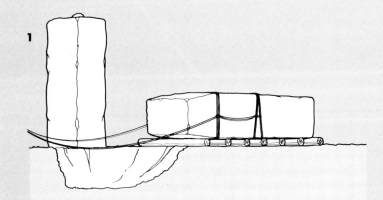

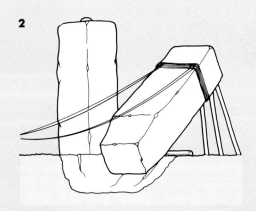

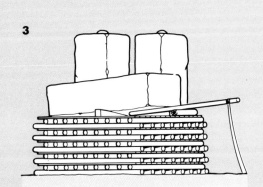

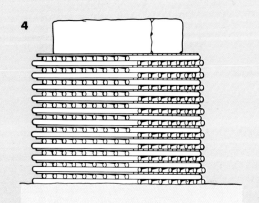

The mammoth task of raising the sarsens at Stonehenge and then dressing them with lintels demanded considerable organizational and engineering skills. Most of the stone came from local sites about 24 miles (40km) away, though some was transported from Prescelly in Wales – a staggering distance of 132 miles (220km).

1 The first step was to dig a foundation pit. One side of the pit was cut in the form of a ramp, so the sarsen could be slid down it to be raised against the facing vertical. This vertical was strengthened with stakes as a precaution against crushing the chalk wall. The sarsen was then hauled to the edge of the pit on log rollers.

2 Once the sarsen had reached the pit, it was levered upwards until it overbalanced to slide into the pit.

3 The sarsen was then hoisted into its final vertical position. An elaborate framework of timber scaffolding, levers and struts were used, backed up by the muscle power of labourers hauling on ropes.

4 A similar timber scaffolding was used to raise the lintel into position.

■ the greeks

Greek architecture is the most important and influential in Western history. Reaching a peak between 400 and 300 B.C. it was developed, some would say vulgarized, by the Romans and then absorbed into the Byzantine.

The Egyptian palaces and temples were built for the satisfaction of priests and royalty; the public at large never penetrated these sanctuaries. Greek society, however, was totally inclusive and stone was used for structures covering uses that reflected a much wider and more open society in which literature, music, drama and sport thrived.

It is a relief to turn to Greek architecture. The contrast in freedom and sanity after the Egyptian style is evident in all their buildings. This architecture too appears to have developed from wooden buildings; a translation as it were, of carpentry technology into stone. Thus, the well-known motifs in Greek Classical stone construction had their origin, as did the capitals in Egyptian architecture, in nature. The basic components of the construction were the stepped podium or stylobate (the base to the column), the column or shaft itself, the capital, and the entablature, (the horizontal member at roof level). At either end above the entablature was the triangular form of the pediment. All the timber clips, pegs and notches of the original timber construction were replicated in stonework, embellished and decorated to give the finished building a precisely detailed refinement.

These components were developed in three modes known as "the orders": Doric, Ionic and Corinthian. The principal difference between them can be seen in the capitals, although there were minor differences in the entablature as well as the fluting to the column. The simplest, most widespread and famous order was the Doric, with the cushion-like profile to the capital making a comfortable junction with the vertical shaft beneath and horizontal lintel above. The evolution and refinement of Classical Greek architecture that took place over this intense period of building activity can be examined by comparing the details of the capitals on the Basilica (c.530 B.C.), one of the three well-preserved temples at Paestum in southern Italy, with the most famous of all Greek temples, the Parthenon (447–432 B.C.), on the Acropolis in Athens. In the earlier building, the profile of the column and capital is clearly exaggerated. These same components become slimmer, more subtle and apparently more at peace with one another, as seen in the outline at the Parthenon. It is worth noting that such was the skill of the Greek masons that in some instances base, column and capital were made of one piece of stone. The second order, the Ionic, emanating from Asia Minor, introduced capitals with a scroll on the inner and outer faces. This endowed the column with a back, front and sides, giving it an axis for direction. The last and most complex of the orders was the Corinthian, whose capitals sprouted in an organic flourish of leaves.

The mathematical module of all these Classical compositions was the diameter of the column measured at one-third of the height from its base. The columns of the temple at Paestum were four modules high and those of the Parthenon six modules high, relative proportions that illustrate the gradual slimming down of the Doric column.

ABOVE The three orders of Greek architecture were Doric, Ionic and Corinthian. The first two developed simultaneously in different parts of the Greek world, the Corinthian order was a later development, which greatly influenced the Romans. The Doric column (centre) is unique in having no base. The shaft is fluted, while the capital, or crowning feature, is plain. The Ionic column (right) is slimmer and more elegant. Its distinguishing feature is the *volutes* (scrolls or spirals) that decorate the capital. The capital of the Corinthian column (*left*) is bell-shaped, while the volutes are supported by eight acanthus leaves. Doric shafts are always fluted, the other two orders generally follow the same style.

LEFT Olympia, Greece (450 B.C.). Entrance to the stadium, site of the first Olympic Games. Greek columns were made up of drums so meticulously constructed that they fitted together without the need of mortar. Central dowels of wood or iron were used to keep them in position.

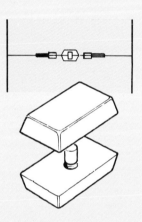

ABOVE The jointing method for a Doric column involved square inserts in the centre of each block, joined with a pin. Lifting bosses to aid positioning of each block would be cut off when the building was complete.

LEFT Temple of Zeus, Selinunte, Sicily (540 B.C.). Detail of Doric capitals shows the simple concave fluting which lends grace to the otherwise stocky column.

LEFT The Temple of Poseidon, Paestum (**FAR LEFT**) is a well-preserved example of early Hellenic architecture, though the plan is still long and the proportions rather heavy. The Parthenon, Athens (**LEFT**) shows how style became refined. A unifying feature of the two buildings is the even number of columns, hence the uneven number of bays.

ABOVE The nobility of the Parthenon is unmistakeable. Built at the top of a hill overlooking Athens, between 447 and 432 B.C., it was intended as the finest temple in Greece. It was wider and longer than any other temple of the time, built out of marble, as no other Doric temple had been before, and richly endowed with sculpture. The precision of the masonry is demonstrated by the almost imperceptible dry joints. Each marble block was worked to key in with the next.

The art of architecture throughout the Western world has never been disengaged from the theory and practice concentrated upon the construction of Greek temples between 700 and 500 B.C. Buildings of apparent simplicity, the Greek temples embodied a development that unfolded over 200 years, and resulted in the highest refinement of technique and proportion.

Greek temples were designed to house either a figurative or a symbolic figure, or an oracle. The composition of elements that we see on the exterior of a Greek temple is a direct reflection of the organization of the interior space in relation to the exterior loggia. This loggia or portico was devised to prepare the visitor for entry. It is thought that the long colonnades on either side running back from this loggia were also to help protect the inner cellular wall to the main hall, constructed of mud in the early temples, from the intense heat of the sun. Egyptian temples had internal columns and exterior walls; Greek temples had internal walls surrounded by columns.

As Greek architecture presents the peak of pure abstract design, then its greatest single masterpiece was the Parthenon, built, or rather rebuilt, after destruction by the Persians, in about 440 B.C. This temple, which housed the golden statue of the virgin Athena, is the dominant building of the Acropolis, a group of temples built on a hill outside Athens. The sophistication of its geometry is legendary. The columns are bowed outwards slightly to avoid the impression of instability. Likewise the outer columns incline inwards, so gently that it has been calculated that their projected meeting point would be a kilometre or so above the temple. There is barely a straight line anywhere. Down below was the Agora, a meeting place of markets, shops and small temples. Here Pericles spoke and Plato, Aristotle and Socrates wandered and talked, and presided over the birth of Western culture.

Below the Acropolis, on the other side from the Agora, was built the theatre of Dionysius which seated 30,000. Although the Greeks, like the Egyptians, were not structurally innovative, their technology was nevertheless astonishing, and the words of the actors and chorus could be heard from every seat, although there was no roof and probably only a light wooden structure behind the stage to reflect sound back at the audience.

The majority of early Greek temples were constructed from Parian marble. This had a smooth, hard and creamy consistency, it could be tooled easily on either axis, and was capable of taking a fine polish. Later, from about 500 B.C. onwards, stone was quarried from the Pentelic Mountains, more readily accessible to Athens.

The precision with which the stones were cut and laid would be a match for us today. The faces of the stone pieces which abutted one another were dressed to be concave, facilitating the close fitting of the hairline joints on the exposed faces of the stone. In this manner, the stones were so exactly matched that they were set with dry joints – without any additional setting agent to fill the gap between the stones.

Later, the pieces of stone were mechanically coupled one to another by a metal tie of bronze, or more usually iron, which was set in dovetail pockets on either face of the stone joint. These ties would then be set in position with molten lead.

■ the romans

Greek architecture spread along the sea route of the Mediterranean and temples are found in Sicily and Southern Italy. But the younger empire of Rome was by now expanding through sheer military and strategic energy and genius. Having absorbed the nearby Etruscans, whose architectural technology they took over, the small state of Rome quickly overran the whole of Italy. Sicily and North Africa followed and by the time of Julius Caesar, the Roman Empire stretched from Northumberland to Egypt, from Spain to Mesopotamia.

Their architecture reflects the extraordinary engineering inventiveness and public self-esteem and aggrandizement of the new empire. The Roman Forum was very different from the more cultivated Agora: it was an arena for public spectacle and games and contests of all kinds. Public buildings, thermal baths and stadia took precedence over temples, the Romans taking their religion more lightly than the Greeks – the most important deities being, in any case, household divinities. The Romans took religion, like architecture, from the Greeks but recast both to suit an extrovert and materialistic way of life. Little wonder that they favoured the Corinthian order, with all its possibilities for elaboration and display.

The Roman temple in general character is similar to the Greek, but the open porch or colonnade is positioned at the front on the axis of the entrance. Steps lead up to the colonnade on the front face only. The sides or flanks are blind, and the walls are modulated by half-columns or pilasters.

Superficially Roman architecture was simpler in detail, and on a larger, more robust, scale than the delicate buildings of the Greeks. It is characterized by the large open structures built at the height of the Roman Empire. The Romans also gave their buildings a richer mix of detail. Although the arch was not unknown to the Greeks, it was the Romans who exploited this Etruscan invention. The circle, semicircle and half-sphere became the principle geometric figures upon which Roman architecture was based.

The Romans, as well as adopting and in some cases bowdlerizing the Greek orders, also adopted the triangular profile of the pediment, revealing the principle of structural rigidity resulting from triangulation. The base chord becomes a tension member, which, together with the angled compression members, constitutes a truss.

Roman stonework, more inventive, more alert to engineering principles, was coarser in comparison to Greek stonework. The Romans made use of dressed facings, frequently relying on concrete to provide structural integrity and rubble to provide mass. The skeleton work was made of stone, brick and tile which held the rougher sandwich infill construction together.

The Romans had access to a wide range of building materials – terracotta, brick, stone and marble – but their most significant innovation in the art of building was the development of concrete – pozzolana – which was used extensively as the structural core of buildings. Brick, stone and marble were all used as facing materials, either added later or sometimes built first to provide permanent shuttering for the plastic concrete.

The Roman building programme was formidable in both scope and complexity and they learnt how to combine materials to exploit the best qualities of each. For the Colosseum (A.D. 70–82), lava was used for the solid foundations, tufa and brick for the supporting walls and lightweight pumice stone in the vaults. The Pantheon (A.D. 120–124) also demonstrates an interesting mix of materials. The dome is a hemisphere, the inner surface of which is coffered in five ranges. It has been established that the dome was constructed from brickwork with thick mortar laid in horizontal courses up to the fourth range of coffers and also around the central opening at the summit.

The Romans established brickmaking wherever they found plentiful supplies of clay. Their bricks look more like large tiles, rarely more than 1½ inches (4 cm) thick and 18 × 9 inches (46 × 23 cm) on plan. They are well-burnt and therefore durable. This shape grew out of the uses which they made of the material – as bonding courses in rubble walls, relieving arches in composite vaults, and for voussoirs (the wedge-shaped blocks making an arch).

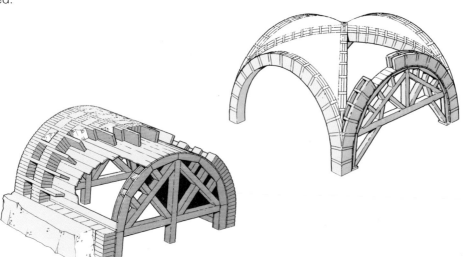

LEFT The Romans built cross-vaults over square apartments, long halls or corridors. The cross-vault was formed from the intersection of two semicircular vaults, equal in span. The lines of intersection are known as "groins".

FAR LEFT First developed in Roman times, the barrel vault has remained a major building form. Temporary timber frame – "centering" – supported the vault, which was made of bricks filled with concrete. Brick tiles were also used to face the arch, as voussoirs.

TOP Aqueduct at Segovia (Roman, A.D. 10). The design of aqueducts and bridges is normally considered the province of engineers. However, these types of structures have profoundly affected architectural design. The curved arch, usually associated with the architect-engineers of the Roman Empire, was able to span greater distances than the lintel and column methods of Greek construction. Here, the arches are supported on simple piers and the overall impression is one of function rather than decoration.

ABOVE Colosseum, Rome (A.D. 70–82). The most magnificent of all Roman amphitheatres and the first to be built entirely above ground, instead of making use of natural contours or terraced hillsides. It is elliptical in plan with seating for 50,000 spectators, and constructed of a series of radiating wedge-shaped buttresses. These were pierced at intervals to permit lateral corridors, which support sloping concrete vaults, and these in turn carry the tiers of seating. An elaborate network of internal access routes and staircases leads out on to the terraces. In the lowest chambers, at ground level, were caged the wild animals used in combat. The curved outer wall has four arched tiers, originally faced in marble.

■ after the romans: the byzantines

Of the Romans' spectacular engineering skill, much has survived. The Romans were the first to lay down roads across Europe. Roads needed bridges, sometimes viaducts. They brought water in high aqueducts from the hills into Rome. The first large domed building, the Pantheon, was built. As the empire failed, when the huge territories could no longer be defended from barbarians from the North, their democracy and technology withered too. In A.D. 324, the Christian Emperor Constantine moved East and made his seat in modern-day Istanbul.

The main building material in Constantinople, mud, was made into bricks and tiles. The techniques of construction and the geometry of space were more Eastern than Western. Earlier buildings were plundered, and the components incorporated into new structures.

Hagia Sophia (532 B.C.), built by Justinian, was the first square volume space to be capped by a dome. The geometrical reconciliation of square and circle was absorbed by "pendentives", the triangular void between the arches and the underside of the circular plan. The massive and homogeneous nature of the church expresses no one material more than another. The colossal piers are stone and the dome is brick. The surfaces have been covered successively with paint, marble and mosaic, not as an illumination of structure, but for religious decorative purposes.

Byzantine churches proliferated throughout Asia Minor, relying on an arrangement of clay domes supported on stone piers. The roofs of all other major spaces constructed at this time were timber, but it was in north Italy that the construction of basilicas first made use of the Roman barrel vault. In order to facilitate light entering the space spanned by the principal barrel vault, secondary vaults were introduced at right-angles to the main space, the junction between the two vaults being known as the groin vault.

The Emperor Justinian (527–565) established centres in Ravenna and Sicily where churches combining the old basilica form with the new Byzantine ones are to be found. Greek architects built Saint Mark's cathedral in Venice, which had become a Byzantine trading outpost. About this time, Byzantium itself began to decline, succumbing finally to the Turks in 1453, whereupon the centre of power swung back again to the western Mediterranean.

■ the anglo-saxon period

The timber building tradition in Britain can be used as a yardstick by which to measure and compare the achievements, in Western architectural terms, of other regions. This is chiefly due to the fact that the quality, antiquity, progressive development and variety of application of surviving buildings is greater in Britain than anywhere else: only in Norway are there a few complete examples which are older.

The timber building tradition in Britain was conceived during what is loosely referred to as the Anglo-Saxon period. This was a time of widespread upheaval which extended from the end of the Iron Age, through the Roman occupation (which had surprisingly little lasting influence on building) to the tenth century, by which time the splendid wooden buildings of England had few rivals in Europe and maybe even in the world.

Archaeological evidence is the only means of determining the size and form of the timber buildings of the post-Roman period, but excavations of royal sites at Yeavering and Cheddar give a fairly accurate picture of the structure of the barn-like "long houses" and the aisled halls of the wealthy landowners prior to the Norman Conquest. Although the aisled halls of the late Saxons are often stated

LEFT San Apollinare Nuovo, Ravenna, Italy (490). The intricate nave arcading supports a plain wall decorated with mosaic saints. High windows, called clerestories, throw light down into the nave. The roof is simple and flat.

ABOVE San Apollinare in Classe, Ravenna, Italy (534). A typical basilica church, deriving from Roman secular architecture. The exterior is of simple brick with tiled roofs, and the composition is set off against a round campanile, or bell tower.

LEFT This parish church at Greensted, Essex, has been dated A.D. 845. Originally a temporary building put up to house the body of St Edmund on its way to a burial place at Bury St Edmund's, the roof was later replaced and reconstruction carried out. The stave walls and gable ends remain of the original shrine, with corner joints of log cabin construction. It is thought that many of the logs used in the vertical staving may have come from the same 600-year-old oak.

as having their origins on the European mainland, evidence suggests that the 89-foot (27 m) long aisled hall at Yeavering is a regional type. Its walls were built of squared timbers set upright in a foundation trench with no sill or sleeper beams – closely related structures are known to have existed in the Northumbrian region which date from a period when this area was controlled by the Celts.

Only one wooden church survives from this period, and it is in a mutilated state. It is at Greensted in Essex and is distinguished by its walls of ancient timbers placed vertically side by side. These "stave-walls" are a feature of the richly decorated mast-churches of Norway.

The Norman Conquest brought the influence of Byzantium to Britain but the European tradition persisted in native timber structures. It is not generally realized that many of the motte and bailey castles of the early Normans were not the complicated stone structures usually associated with this period but often consisted of a wooden building atop a mound with a palisaded court. The carpenters' skills were still important for flooring and roofing the mighty stone keeps, which date from the time of the

Crusades. There are remains of halls from the twelfth century – the Bishop's Palace at Farnham and the Bishop's Hall at Hereford are two examples – but little survives which can be ascribed to this period with any confidence.

The thirteenth century saw the last of the aisled halls, as stone succeeded timber.

RIGHT Detail of one of the dome systems used in Hagia Sophia. Structural intricacy with arches, domes and semi-domes does not detract from the overall simplicity of design. The main dome is constructed entirely of bricks, covered internally with plaster and decorated with shimmering mosaic.

■ romanesque architecture

FOR SOME REASON THE ITALIANS remained wedded to their own basilica plan which they now elaborated with white and coloured marbles so that their churches came to resemble decorated ivory jewel boxes. They also developed a style of surface arcading which they built up, tier upon tier, to cover the entire facade, as at Pisa. The famous leaning tower, or campanile, is simply a hollow column of arcades, architecturally reflecting the walls of the cathedral close by.

This style, known as Romanesque, in which the round-headed arch became prominent, spread from Italy to France and Germany, eventually reaching Britain (where it is generally called Norman) through the invasions of William the Conqueror. Away from Italy the prettiness and refinement fell away. For one thing there was no rich marble to hand and social conditions in the rest of Europe were so precarious that castles were needed to protect the populace from wandering marauders. Indeed, many churches, and even cathedrals such as Albi, were built as fortresses and acted as sanctuaries for their congregations in troubled times.

Nevertheless the use of simple, if sometimes crude, ornament persisted, as can be seen in the great churches of Vézelay in France and Durham in England. Their architects loved bold geometric patterns of all kinds, and chevrons, zig-zags, dog toothing and stripes decorate their churches. They also incorporated naturalistic carving which, while primitive in execution, is often direct in its appeal.

Structurally, Romanesque is notable for its mass, its aesthetic is monumental, its structure conservative. The round arch dominates everything, repeated again and again, from huge spans across naves to decorative arcading high up in the triforium (gallery). Roofs were barrel-vaulted or simply cross-vaulted with structural ribs. Nearby older buildings were often ransacked for materials: marbles from ancient Rome were fitted haphazardly into the facades at Pisa and Roman tiles into the masonry of St Albans Abbey.

LEFT St Mary Church, Iffley, Oxford, England (1175). This little church has much in common with contemporary churches in Normandy. The structure is simple and the repeated use of the Roman arch and arcade provides the architectural character of the facade.

ABOVE Salisbury Cathedral, England (1220–60). A classic English cathedral, both in detail and setting. The west front, though decorated, compared with the French is flat, almost unassuming. French cathedrals of the time were generally placed in the centre of towns and presented a rich and powerful west front with deeply recessed doorways encrusted with sculpture and decoration. Monastic features at Salisbury include decorated cloisters. The eight-sided building is topped by the tallest spire in England (123m/406ft).

▶ british gothic styles

British Gothic architecture is generally divided into three imprecisely defined categories that only roughly correspond to three successive periods in time between 1300 and 1500. However, there are basic differences between the styles.

Early English is characterized by steeply pointed arches above tall, slim openings, often in odd-numbered groups; simple vaulting, commonly with a ridge rib; arch mouldings; secondary columns of marble surrounding main columns; and ball-flower and dogtooth ornamentation.

Decorated style features window tracery in cusped geometrical fashion; heavy and complex mouldings; carved naturalistic ornamentation; and additional ribs in the vaulting.

Perpendicular style is characterized by networks of vertical and horizontal lines in tracery and ornamentation; increased light through the enlargement of window areas; and decorative vaulting ribs, leading eventually to carved traceried fan vaults.

■ british gothic

Although "Gothic" derives from "Goth", a term of abuse which referred to barbarians, we understand this label to refer particularly to that lofty range of north European buildings built between the tenth and fourteenth centuries. Gothic architecture was total in the sense that the visible sinew-like shafts of stone are actually performing the role of support and are not simply a representation of that load-carrying role.

It is difficult to be precise about the moment that Romanesque developed into fully-fledged Gothic. Historians also argue over whether the French or the British were first to erect a true Gothic structure. In France, Abbot Suger (1081–1151) prompted the construction of the St. Denis abbey in 1144, but in Britain, Durham Cathedral, which is strictly Romanesque showing some Gothic characters, was begun in 1093. France and England developed similar but not identical traditions of construction.

The Gothic period saw the development of inventive and innovative techniques exploiting the characteristics of stone. Stone was not simply used on a grand scale to its fullest capacity to create space; the stones were shaped, formed and profiled to produce a fabric which, by use of tracery, virtually became dematerialized.

Pointed vaulting was the key discovery of French and English Gothic architecture. Ribs and shafts, the essential components of the Gothic arcade, ran together in an almost continuous composition whose objectives were to make the fabric as light as possible. An old Indian proverb says, "the arch never sleeps": the arch is always pressing out as well as down. The Gothic vault originated in the intersection of two barrel vaults. It was the introduction of the rib at the intersection of the two barrel vaults which led to the development of the pointed transverse arch. The development of the pointed arch brought great advantages – first, an adjustable geometry was possible as ribbed vaults of different spans could be arranged to meet one another at their crowns; second, where the resulting descending faces were more vertical than horizontal, the weight could be carried to ground level without too great a horizontal thrust. By introducing a rib at the intersection of the two vaults, it was unnecessary to use complicated "centering" to support the vaults during construction. Once positioned, the ribs formed the bones of the structure, upon which the "voussoirs", or vaulting panels, could then be placed.

As with ancient Greek temples, Gothic cathedrals were continuously refined over a period of time – in this case, 500 years. English cathedrals developed in several distinct stages from the robust and monolithic character of Romanesque beginnings, through Early English, Decorated and Perpendicular. The use of stone became increasingly economical and the fabric of enclosure more transparent, with less flat masonry. The use of ribs to break up flat plains of masonry became more intense. The patterns of ribs and panels became finer and more intricate. The fan vaulting of the Perpendicular period was a riot of geometry in which its extrovert, over-developed complexity lost the clarity and dignity of the Early English period.

ABOVE AND RIGHT Chapel, King's College, Cambridge. The medieval metaphysics of light, particularly as interpreted by Abbot Suger of St. Denis, linked the neo-platonic idea of the "oneness" and "luminous aliveness" of the world, with Christian dogma in medieval thought. God as creator of the universe became known as the "superessential light" and Christ as "the first radiance". Suger interpreted these references to light literally and soon the new concept was adopted by others. In northern Europe, the desire for greater light, for religious and for practical reasons, was allied with a development in masonry construction which permitted larger spans. Walls became infills to the structure and were composed of brightly coloured windows supported by delicate traceries of stone.

ABOVE Wells Cathedral, England (1180–1425). A fine, richly decorated Early English nave, terminating with the curious scissor-like bracing at the crossing. The Early English west front is richly arcaded. Its impact derives from its setting among lawns a little way from the town centre.

RIGHT Notre Dame, Paris (1163–1250). View of the south transept. The facades were elaborated in imitation of the first Gothic church, St. Denis. Notre Dame is the last of these early Gothic churches to have galleries above the aisles. The style of the facade was copied throughout France.

■ gothic in europe

From the ninth century onwards, following the decline of the Roman Empire, there was a considerable growth both in secular and ecclesiastical building throughout Europe. In France, the Abbey of St. Denis was a major religious centre, the focus of pilgrimages to the shrine of the patron saint of France, and the burial place of the French kings. By 1124, it was exempt from feudal and ecclesiastical domination and subject only to the king.

The Abbot of St. Denis, Suger, a brilliant and energetic organizer, was also a flamboyant opportunist who saw a way of attracting still more custom to his church by reconstructing the building. Suger loved splendour and while he knew it would appeal to the pilgrims and to the king, his patron, he was afraid that the church would object to his extravagance. Consequently, he justified his expenditure by referring to the medieval metaphysics of light. In medieval thought, the universe was unified by "the superessential light" or "invisible sun", with God the Father as "the father of the lights".

Suger interpreted the metaphysical references to light in Christian dogma quite literally, and quickly set about rebuilding St. Denis as a monumental expression of this vision. Rejecting the Romanesque architecture of the time, he brought in craftsmen from abroad and began reconstructing his church with much larger windows and with bright stained glass to instruct the pilgrims.

Soon this new concept of light and space was adopted by others, first in France and then elsewhere throughout Europe. It fitted well with the northern climate with its dark winters and consequent need for larger apertures to let in light. As the craftsmen gained confidence with stone, churches sprang up ever more daring and lighter.

Churches no longer had to be fortified. The new technology in stone, achieved largely by trial and error, meant buildings now reached astonishing heights. By means of transferring the outward thrust of the new roof vaults to flying buttresses, which were outside the building, walls could be virtually hung with glass. Churches, like Ste Chappelle in Paris and Chartres Cathedral, became like glass houses where Bible stories, warnings of damnation or veneration of local saints could be depicted in glass cartoons for an enthusiastic, if largely illiterate, population.

The fervour and excitement of Gothic architecture needs to be experienced in the buildings themselves. Even so, their increasing survival as museums today dilutes the impact they must have had in the Middle Ages.

ABOVE Milan Cathedral, Italy (1385–1485). The last great flowering of European Gothic. Milan was actually completed after the first Renaissance buildings had been built in Florence. Considered "debased" Gothic by some, few visitors fail to respond to its huge, airy interior or to the glory of this west facade.

RIGHT Chartres Cathedral, France (1194–1260). Earliest example of High Gothic. The entrance, which confronts a small square is simple by French standards. The cathedral's great glories are its sculptured figures and stained glass windows. The quality of their design is unequalled. Nine towers were planned, only two completed: the fine north spire was built in 1506, with no attempt to match the earlier tower to the south (12th century).

LEFT This huge window in the north transept of Chartres consists of a circular rose above five simple lancets. It is a magnificent resolution of stone geometry with stained glass artistry.

■ medieval woodcraftsmanship

The carpenter really emerged again in the fourteenth century, when the embryonic middle class started to assert itself. Unable to afford the luxury of building in stone and hiring masons, this new class resorted to the cheaper and more readily available timber and the services of professional builders. These "yeomen", as the new class may be termed, embarked on a vast building programme which tested the village wrights to the limit of their craft. The wrights were forced to emulate the multistorey, rigid stone-built structures of the establishment. The only way this could be achieved was to develop methods of tying or "trussing" the rafters of the roof in such a way that they stiffened the stud frame wall panels, whose resistance to overturning was so much less than the stone walls of the great houses. The lap-dovetail tying joints of this period are probably the finest of their type, and they were used at ends of buildings and at intermediate bays of 12 to 16 feet (3.5 to 5 m) depending upon the scale of the structure, where main posts occurred. At these bay points trusses were formed to tie and support pairs of larger rafters, so that longitudinal members could be carried, which in turn supported the smaller common rafters. The bay pattern was usually consistent through all floors of the building. The smaller rafters were set in pairs, joined at the top and about midway down their span, by a horizontal tying member called a collar. Longitudinally beneath this and on the centre line of the roof, ran a timber bearer which was supported on the midpoint of each tie beam by a crown-post — often carved and decorated and with a cluster of curved braces at its top to add further rigidity to the roof.

Floor joists were laid "flat-on" and it is often said that this fact, coupled with the application of the cantilever principle, led to the appearance of that most characteristic of Tudor features — the jetty. This was an essential feature of what is now called platform framing — or the framing of each storey separately and setting one on top of the other. By jettying certain parts of the building only, a great variation in elevational treatment could be obtained — for instance, the Kentish farmhouse style with its external curved braces. Elaborately carved oriel windows were introduced beneath the overhangs, and roof-shapes were often deliberately complex.

To carry the jetty around an angle (perhaps at the corner of two streets), a diagonal beam was introduced across the corner bay and projected out over the top of a carved corner post (teazle post). This beam is known as a dragon beam. The name is thought to be a corruption of "diagonal", but it may also be the result of Japanese influence.

In fifteenth- and sixteenth-century Europe, as now, the tallest buildings generally were in the towns. Their similarity of form was to some extent controlled by limitation of plot size and the building constraints of the period. The ground

floor was usually partly open for use as a shop, while the merchant occupier and his family lived above. There were no models for the public buildings which this urban life demanded, so schools, assembly halls and inns took on similar form to domestic buildings. The inn, however, soon developed its own style as a direct result of the need for stabling: the double front with gated archway and internal courtyard is ubiquitous.

Native forms of wholly wooden buildings continued in barns, mills and sail lofts. Of these, water mills are the most striking. These buildings were essentially functional with little or no decoration, built of half-timber framing, but with larger members and closer bay patterns than houses to deal with the increased loads. Gravity was used for grain handling and the projecting hoist housing or "lucum" became the universally distinguishing feature of the superstructure.

At the edges of towns where commercial change had made speculative development a viable proposition, rows of terrace houses appeared – sometimes a dozen or more in a row. The best examples are what would now be called "narrow-frontage" and with a continuous jetty over the pavement, they have a simplicity of form and aesthetic discipline which is equalled only by the best practitioners today.

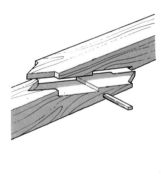

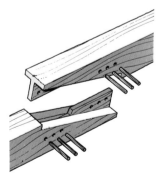

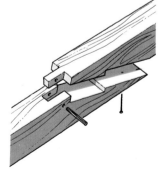

LEFT Trunch Church, Norfolk, England (c1500). Fine Perpendicular ceiling in this parish church displays the ingenuity and craftsmanship with which East Anglian carpenters sought to elaborate their roof trusses.

ABOVE Various types of English scarf joints from the thirteenth and fourteenth centuries. Since different joints attained perfection at different periods, studying joints can be a useful way of dating timber buildings.

■ medieval brickwork

Bricks and brickwork do not play a major role in the development of Gothic from the Romanesque in the twelfth century, although it is significant that where there were supplies of brick, it was used to reproduce the forms which history suggests were the preserve of stone. The Lombardy plain in north Italy has churches built from local brick, although this is an area in which the Roman traditions were strong. The Cathedral at Albi (1282–1390) is a fortress church built in brick. It is a simple plan, containing one major vaulted space and an apsidal end. The brickwork walls undulate as the internal buttresses register on the external skin. Brick is well suited to this form of expression and the whole building is a powerful composition.

The most extensive use of brick was in the Netherlands and north Germany and, once more, it was the lack of building stone and the availability of clay which promoted the material. What is not clear is how or where the art of brickmaking was rediscovered in Europe. It is generally held that brickmaking in Europe ceased with the collapse of the Roman Empire and did not start again until the middle of the thirteenth century. There were strong trading links between the towns of the Hanseatic League (a league formed by German merchants at home and abroad for the defence of their trading interests) and Venice, so it is conceivable that the brick builders of the coastal towns of the Netherlands and northern Germany could have learnt from some eastern source, or perhaps from Lombardy. Whatever the reason, the Flemish, Dutch and north German

ABOVE Tattershall Castle, Lincolnshire (1433–50). A random disposition of the window openings is possible in brick construction. The effect here is more fortified than at Oxburgh Hall.

RIGHT Queen's College, Cambridge (1448–9). As a contrast to the planar quality of the brickwork in Oxburgh Hall, here the thickness of the walls is shown in the depth of the window openings.

trading partners of the Hanseatic League were instrumental in nurturing and spreading the skills of brickmaker and bricklayer. Lubeck Cathedral was a north German Romanesque building which was begun in 1173 and received Gothic additions in 1335. Both stages of the building were executed in brickwork, which was even used for the window mullions and tracery. Other major brick buildings were built in the town of Lubeck, and it is certain that the work provided a stimulus for the development of brickwork building in England.

Many towns and ports in England were members of the Hanseatic League, notably York, Hull, Boston, Yarmouth, London and Bristol, so it was in the east and southeast that brickwork began to flourish. The raw material was available, the skill to exploit it arrived with immigrants from Flanders and the Netherlands during power struggles in the thirteenth and fourteenth centuries, and the desire to use it had been fostered by the northern European examples.

In the twelfth century, Roman bricks had been quarried from existing structures and incorporated in new buildings, especially around St. Albans and Colchester, but the earliest domestic brick building in England is probably Little Wenham Hall, Suffolk. It is a brick structure dating from the end of the thirteenth century, L-shaped in plan, with a tower and turret stair in the inside corner. The bricks differ in size and colour and they are used in conjunction with limestone for the dressings and windows. The bricks were burnt on the site and it is thought that the expertise was provided by Flemish brickmakers.

It was obviously sound practice, given the limitations of transport, to make bricks for a building as close to the site as possible. Many buildings were built from brick fields which were exploited for that building alone. However, in 1303, Hull established a municipal brickworks, and land at Beverley was leased for brickmaking. These two operations were obviously designed to allow Hull to compete with its Hanseatic partners.

Hull was England's first brick-built town. It was a fortified town laid out on a grid plan, but all that remains today is the original centrepiece of the town – the Church of Holy Trinity. Local brick was used to construct the chancel and transepts (1315–45), while the nave and upper portion of the tower were built of stone. As at Little Wenham, stone was used for the dressings and windows. Beverley Minster, in the nearby market town of Beverley, has a vault of brickwork with stone ribs, and North Bar (1409), the only survivor of Beverley's gates, is a three-storeyed brick structure with some interesting details – three blank niches on the south front and a dentilated string-course under the battlements.

Henry VI used brick at Greenwich and Richmond Palaces, but his most extensive use of the material was at Eton College. The College was founded in 1440 and, although the Chapel walls are stone, the rest is built from bricks which were made from clay deposits at Slough. Three million bricks were supplied to the site between 1442 and 1452. Bishop Waynflete, the first Headmaster of Eton, was also an enthusiastic builder. He added a brick-built tower to the stone castle at Farnham and built a palace at Esher from which only the water-gate tower survives. He founded Magdalen College, Oxford in 1458, but followed local tradition and built in stone.

ABOVE One of the enduring symbols of Tudor brickwork, the exuberant, decorative chimneys express the enthusiasm of their builders.

Three other bishops, Rotherham, Fisher and Alcock, each of whom was Bishop of Rochester at some time in his career, were instrumental in the foundation of four Cambridge colleges. Rotherham was a founder of Queen's College (1448–9), Alcock founded Jesus (1500), Fisher organised the building of Christ's (1505–11) and St. John's (1511) on behalf of the foundress, Lady Margaret de Beaufort. Brick was used in all four colleges. Although they are now obscured at Christ's, the gateways and their attached ranges are fine examples of the skill of the Tudor builders.

The brick-built gateway and courtyard form recurs at Oxburgh Castle, Norfolk (1482), a moated house with a spectacular gate tower rising 70 feet (21 m) from the moat. The tower is surrounded by polygonal turrets, between which there are crow-stepped gables and machicolations.

Tattershall Castle, Lincolnshire (1433–50) was built by Ralph Cromwell, Treasurer to Henry VI; although only the Tower House survives, it is a powerful piece of brick building, five storeys – 110 feet (34 m) – high. The interior is finished in brick and contains four noteworthy chimneypieces made of limestone.

5 the renaissance

■ the beginnings: neo-classicism

FILIPPO BRUNELLESCHI (1377–1446) is said to have founded the Renaissance style of architecture. Architecture was a major part of the flourishing of the arts generally, a tide that swept northwards from Florence in the mid-fifteenth century.

The Renaissance was characterized by artists, town planners and musicians, all involved in a quest for the ideal. A search for refinement, a preoccupation with symmetry and the study of the relationships between light and dark, solid and void, and the general belief in the visual and spiritual advantages of harmony, became the bases of Renaissance architecture. Mathematical systems furnished formulas for studies in the proportion of objects. Similar analysis was used for establishing relationships between objects and buildings. This led to a greater comprehension of the phenomenon of perspective and the techniques for portraying it. The proportion of the human body also took on a renewed significance and proportional lessons were drawn from it.

The writings and lessons of Vitruvius, who was a Roman architect and engineer of the first century B.C. were reexamined. An architectural vocabulary taken from classical forms and the systems to which it referred became the basis of Renaissance inventiveness. The classical measurements and ideals were used in a new series of compositional relationships and prompted the appearance of a new professional class of builders, described as architectects. The architectural furniture of the Renaissance included the classical column, the pediment, the entablature, the Roman arch and the podium, and what was to become known as the "piano nobile". This was the name of the first floor of Italian palaces where the main apartments were located.

Churches, palaces and organized open, urban spaces are the architectural works most often associated with this time. Great skill was exercised in ordering the interior of buildings, frequently using the same motifs as had been traditionally associated with the exterior. The ordering of the exterior was a separate problem, solved by taking into account abstract considerations.

Whereas Gothic architecture was a direct expression of structure, the stonework of the Renaissance developed into contrived derivations of authentic Classicism. Although stone played a part in furnishing the architecture of the Renaissance, it was habitually used as a dressing material and not in a strictly functional sense. It was frequently used simply as ornamental infill, such as on the main facade of Santa Maria Novella in Florence (1456–70) which was designed by Leon Battista Alberti (1404–72). Stone facings were added to walls frequently built of nothing more than rubble; exceptions were the Palazzo Riccardi (1444) by Michelozzi (1396–1472) and the Palazzo Rucellai (1466) by Alberti. In Palazzo Ricardi, the detail of stone is given exaggerated definition to illustrate the differences between the much fortified wall of the ground floor, the public floor, and the open formal rooms on the first floor or piano nobile. Although the ultimate Renaissance architect, Andrea Palladio (1508–80) used the motifs of stonework, his buildings were mainly built of stucco. As with late Gothic architecture, the designs of the Renaissance became over-developed, eventually adopting forms that were later known as Baroque.

ABOVE Ospedale degli Innocenti, Florence, Italy (Brunelleschi 1419–44). Trained as a goldsmith, Brunelleschi was also a great sculptor and engineer. This simple and elegant hospice is one of the first true Renaissance buildings. The colonnade is of Corinthian columns supporting arcading, which is decorated with ceramic plaques by Luca della Robbia.

LEFT The dome of Florence Cathedral, Italy (Brunelleschi, 1420–34). This famous competition design was set to find a solution for covering the Gothic octagon of Florence Cathedral. Brunelleschi solved the problem by constructing double shells supported on stone ribs. A heavy lantern crowns the dome. The red-tiled exterior soaring above the roofs of Florence, dominates one of the greatest of all city landscapes.

ABOVE Palais de Fontainebleau, France (1528–40). Gilles le Breton (*fl c*1530). The great courtyard of the Royal Palace shows the haphazard nature of its architectural composition, an informality unthinkable in Italy. A favourite French feature is the steep roof, itself two storeys high and lit by dormers — windows projecting forwards from the slope. Another notable feature is the horseshoe staircase, a double serpentine flight of steps so large it encircles a small courtyard of its own at ground level. Italian palaces closed their faces to the public: those in France did the reverse in a public demonstration of power and authority.

■ the architect as a celebrity

Before this date, the role of the architect had begun to change in northern Italy. We know the names of many Gothic master-masons, and we know how highly regarded they were as masters of their craft, but there was no notion of individual creativity in their culture. However, when Florence appointed the painter Giotto as its master-mason in 1334, a change in the concept of the designer began and, by the mid-fifteenth century, in northern Italy at least, the architect was established as an artist. After 1500, Renaissance ideas spread north, initially to France, and inspired the design of secular buildings such as palaces and town halls, while sacred architecture continued in the Gothic tradition alongside.

The new architects were scholars, no longer master-masons or monks, and the invention of printing spread the new vocabulary more quickly and effectively than by the travelling guildsmen of medieval Europe. The first great treatise, *De Re Aedificatoria* by Alberti, was published in 1485 and remained a standard text book. Alberti had gone back to Greek geometry and rules of proportion, and formulated a set of rules based on the proportions of the human form. In this way buildings could be designed in which no part was less important than another in its relation to the whole.

Alberti was no mere theorist. He built a palace for the Rucellai family in Florence and travelled to carry out works in Mantua and Rimini. Rome was next to succumb. Donato Bramante (1444–1514), a Florentine by birth, went to study there and stayed for the remainder of his life. He was responsible for a small but extremely elegant colonnaded chapel, the Tempietto (1502), which was to have a wider influence in Europe than its size would seem to warrant. On a vaster scale, Bramante prepared the original designs for St. Peter's, but on the death of Pope Julius II, he was dismissed and his plans were superseded by other and lesser architects. Bramante died in 1514, and by this time the Renaissance was well established. The second generation saw a distinct change of mood.

BELOW AND BOTTOM Broughton Castle, Oxfordshire, England (*c*1580). A transitional castle, originally fortified but adapted and extended in quieter times. The general informality is medieval, tempered with the new and only partly understood Classical details imported from Europe. The fireplace in the drawing room, Elizabethan in size and importance, is nevertheless Renaissance in its detailing. So is the panelling, with Classical decorations applied as if by a pastrycook.

▶ alberti

Leon Battista Alberti was born in Genoa in 1404, the illegitimate son of a nobleman who had been exiled from Florence. Educated at Padua and Bologna, he went at the age of 24 to Florence where, as a papal secretary, he came into close contact with the thinkers and the artists of the burgeoning Renaissance. In such intense and creative surroundings, it was he who first determined to write a full account of the new discoveries, the new methods and the new principles, and by virtue of his voracious appetite for knowledge and his skill in expression, his works are as valuable today as they were in his own time.

A friend of the great artists Brunelleschi, Donatello, Ghiberti, Masaccio and Luca della Robbia, Alberti dedicated his first major theoretical work on the arts to them all. Written in Latin (in which Alberti had been fluent since his schooldays), this was *De Pictura*. It was later translated into Italian as *Della Pittura*, and concerned mainly the new methodologies in painting (including perspective).

He also produced a large treatise on education and the ethics of ordinary family life (*Della Famiglia*), another on sculpture (*De Statua*), and other works on religion, jurisprudence, government and politics, mechanics, linguistics, domesticated animals, and mathematics. In all he wrote he was the complete master of the information concerned. He aimed to give a rational and scientific basis for everything he wrote, even when discussing such abstract entities as beauty.

But his most influential opus was on the subject of architecture — *De Re Aedificatoria* — modelled on works by Vitruvius. A major feature of this volume was its insistence on proportion and harmony in construction, intended to create buildings that had a unity of composition. He carried out his theoretical ideas in architectural commissions in Florence, Rimini and Mantua, to great effect.

He died in April 1472 while on a visit to Rome.

ABOVE Sta Maria Novella, Florence, Italy (1458–60). Facade by Alberti. A church built by the Dominicans in 1350 so that its structure is essentially Gothic. In 1460 Alberti provided a Renaissance front in which the old basilica form is resolved by the additions of two huge scrolls, into a unified facade.

FAR LEFT Palazzo Rucellai, Florence, Italy (Alberti, 1446–51). This formidable exterior marked a new departure in palace architecture. The stone facade is severe, with three storeys divided into bays by pilasters — flat columns which protrude only a few centimetres beyond the wall. The apartments are reached from an internal courtyard, a plan which remains popular in Italy to this day.

▶ brunelleschi

Filippo Brunelleschi is generally credited with being the founder of the Renaissance style of architecture. Born in Florence in 1377, he carried out all his major works in that city. His initial training was as a goldsmith, and the knowledge of metallurgy and design that this gave him was later invaluable when he turned his hand to architecture and architectural engineering. He was also an excellent draughtsman (his friend Leon Battista Alberti attributed to him the first mathematical understanding of perspective through the use of a vanishing point), and a sculptor and poet besides.

The design and constructional engineering behind the great dome of Florence Cathedral (Sta Maria del Fiore), carried out in partnership with the sculptor Lorenzo Ghiberti, is often considered Brunelleschi's greatest achievement. His innovatory use of features reflecting the styles of ancient times — particularly monolithic columns and Byzantine-like domes — transformed and enhanced the symmetrical spacing and even lighting that was the late medieval tradition of contemporary Florentine builders.

His first building in a definitively Renaissance style was the Foundling Hospital (Ospedale degli Innocenti) in Florence. He also carried out work in Sta Felicita (the Barbadori Chapel) and Sta Croce (the Pazzi Chapel), and designed the churches of San Lorenzo and Santo Spirito. Though few in number, these projects were each significant, and each progressively showed Brunelleschi's development of a Classical vision of the ideal building.

Among his friends he numbered the famous artists Donatello, Luca della Robbia and Masaccio and the architect and theorist, Alberti. It was solely for Brunelleschi's benefit that Alberti translated his great theoretical work on the arts, *Della Pittura* (1436) from Latin into Italian.

He died in April 1446, and was interred in Florence Cathedral.

BELOW Pazzi Chapel, Florence, Italy (Brunelleschi, 1429). A tiny church built within the cloisters of Santa Croce. Based on Roman temple prototypes, it is, nevertheless, an entirely Renaissance building and one of the most delightful by this great architect.

BELOW Palazzo Pitti, Florence, Italy (Brunelleschi, started 1440). The rough hewn stones of the facade add to the fortified appearance. Note the curiously Florentine detail of Saracenic-shaped arches above the door and window openings. Behind this, on the garden side, the architecture is notably more relaxed.

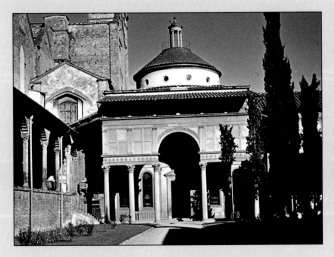

ABOVE Palazzo del Tè, Mantua, Italy. (Giulio Romano, 1525–35). The single storey palazzo is the masterpiece of Giulio Romano, a pupil of Raphael and himself a gifted painter. The courtyard side consists of linked arches forming a graceful colonnade, broken centrally by a deep, shaded portico with simple pediment. The outside of this building, like the great palaces in Florence, presents a prison-like face to the public. The rough stone base, with arches repeating those above, gives stability to the whole composition.

■ michelangelo and italian mannerism

For convenience the Renaissance movement is sometimes divided into Early Renaissance, Mannerism, Baroque and Rococo. The word Mannerism requires an explanation. It has come to describe the reaction to any new style (though strictly speaking it is a Renaissance term), which is deliberately idiosyncratic and often theatrical. Mannerism of a kind can be seen elsewhere, in the late French Gothic for example, and English Decorated. It is also, perhaps, a lazy way of describing an individual talent whose place in architectural history cannot easily be catalogued or slotted into historical sequence. Such a talent was undoubtedly shown by Michelangelo. He came to architecture late in life, as if painting the Sistine Chapel and sculpture had not been enough. His genius as an architect and town planner turned out to be equally great. In the Medici Mausoleum, in which he incorporated his own sculptures of *Night and Day* and *Evening and Dawn*, and in the Laurentian Library it is clear that something new and strange was happening, a twist to classicism which was individual, even wayward, and was to lead others towards the Baroque.

▶ michelangelo

Michelangelo Buonarroti is regarded as one of the most sublime painters and sculptors of all time, yet he was additionally one of the most influential architects and draughtsmen of his day.

He was born in a village in Tuscany in 1475, but moved to Florence at the age of 6. Seven years later he was articled as a painter's apprentice to the Ghirlandaio workshop, despite the disapproval of his father who thought art too lowly an occupation. After only one year, however, he went to learn sculpture under Bertoldo di Giovanni, whose patron was Lorenzo de' Medici, ruler of Florence. The young artist's work was so good that Lorenzo invited him to stay at the palace. There he met many influential thinkers of the Renaissance.

By 1496 Michelangelo had arrived in Rome where he was to carve the two statues that made his name: *Bacchus* (now in the Bargello, Florence) and the *Pietà* (now in St Peter's, Rome). He returned to Florence in 1501 where, soon after, he sculpted his *David*. In 1505 he was in Rome again, summoned by the pope to decorate the ceiling of the Sistine chapel, among other commissions. The ceiling, completed in 1512, established Michelangelo as the foremost painter of his era.

After another brief sojourn in Florence, he settled for good in Rome in 1534. For the next 30 years, working primarily for the papacy, he concentrated his energies mostly on architectural work – such as on parts of the Palazzo Farnese and the Palazzo Senatorio – but in particular on the redesigning and completion of the construction of St. Peter's. Work on St Peter's had come to a virtual standstill after the death of Bramante in 1514. Michelangelo went to work with a will, to the extent that today the exterior of the building (with its notable dome) is said to owe more to him than to any other architect, and to form a fitting conclusion to his titanic career.

Michelangelo died in February 1564, in the presence of a number of friends and doctors. Despite the wish of the pope that he should be buried in St Peter's, his coffin was spirited away to Florence by his nephew and heir, and he was buried there.

RIGHT Palazzo Ducale, Mantua, Italy. (Giulio Romano, 1544). Very different from Giulio Romano's Palazzo del Tè. The courtyard view shows the extraordinary twisted barley-sugar columns of the principal floor.

BELOW St Peter's, Rome (1506–1626). This famous building was destined to be a monument to Pope Julius II who demolished an earlier basilica church on the site to make way for it. Many architects were involved in its eventful history but Bramante, who provided the original Greek cross plan, Michelangelo, who designed its superb dome, and Bernini, who provided the internal visual impact, were the most important.

ABOVE This view of the capital, Rome, from the Palazzo del Senatore, shows the dramatic star-shaped paving at the centre of which Michelangelo placed the ancient Roman bronze statue of Marcus Aurelius.

▶ giulio romano

Giulio de' Gianuzzi was born in Rome (hence the ascription "Romano") probably in 1499. As a child he was apprenticed to the great artist Raphael, whose chief pupil and assistant he rapidly became. Raphael died in 1520, and Giulio took it upon himself to complete several of the master's unfinished works, including the *Transfiguration* in the Vatican. On his own account he also painted several other frescoes in Rome.

But he moved to Mantua in 1524 — just in time to escape possible prosecution for some pornographic drawings — and it was in Mantua that he spent the rest of his life, dominating the artistic affairs of the Gonzaga court.

Probably his greatest work was the design and construction of the Palazzo del Tè, a building meant expressly to flout many of the principles of Classical architecture — and a building designed thus on truly Mannerist lines. In addition Giulio was responsible for much of the interior decoration, and it was as a painter — rather than as an architect — that he was acclaimed in his day: famous enough for Shakespeare to quote his name (but, wrongly, as a sculptor). The house he designed for his own use in Mantua is probably the most important of all his other works.

ABOVE San Giorgio Maggiore, Venice (Palladio, c 1556). The simplicity of this cloister is deceptive, and results from a scrupulous attention to solid and void, embellished with meticulous

architectural ornament. The cool Palladian interior shows the dome over the crossing supported on plain pendentives. The choirs are screened and set off against white plastered wall and vaults.

▶ palladio

Andrea di Pietro della Gondola was born in 1508 in Padua, and was to become possibly the most influential architect of all time. As a child he was apprenticed to a Paduan sculptor, but at the age of 16 he moved to Vicenza where he came under the patronage of the humanist poet and scholar Count Giangiorgio Trissino. It was through Trissino, who was in the act of rebuilding a villa in the ancient Roman style, that Palladio was introduced to the ideas and principles described by Vitruvius more than 1,500 years earlier; he was also introduced to some of the greatest Italian architects of the day, notably Jacopo Sansovino and Alvise Cornaro. It was at this time that he was given the name Palladio, partly in reference to the goddess Pallas, and partly adopting the name of a character in one of Trissino's poems.

His first commissions were for villas and a palace not far from Vicenza in around 1540. The next year he made the first of three visits to Rome, where he absorbed the Renaissance work of artists such as Bramante and Raphael, and studied ancient Roman sculptures and buildings. His first major commission came in 1548, to design the façade of the Town Hall in Vicenza. Thereafter he was forever busy designing palaces of stunning grandeur and villas of exquisite simplicity in and around Vicenza.

Gradually Palladio's work took on some aspects of Mannerism, particularly after he came to know Giulio Romano, who also carried out work in Vicenza. Nonetheless, he always remained true to the mathematical principles outlined by Vitruvius, which he described and popularized in a series of his own textbooks. These reproduced designs not just of buildings but also of bridges, arches and other local amenities. During another visit to Rome in the mid-1550s, Palladio published a book on the antiquities of Rome which became the standard guidebook to the city for the succeeding two centuries.

From 1570, Palladio concentrated on designing churches and monastic buildings in Venice. However, both of his sons died in 1572 and he thereafter lived the life of a recluse. He himself died in 1580, leaving several commissions unfulfilled.

ABOVE Villa Rotonda (or Capra), Vicenza, Italy (Palladio, 1550). Perhaps the most famous villa in the world, certainly one of the most influential. It was copied widely all over Europe, four times in England alone, and the United States. The direct symmetry of the plan can be seen clearly from the corner view. It is constructed in brick which was plastered; stone was restricted to important mouldings and sculpture.

RIGHT Villa Badoer, Rovigo, Italy (Palladio, c 1554). All the hallmarks of this great architect are here: a massive flight of steps leading up to an elegant portico, flanked by bare walls pierced with simple openings. Smallest details of proportion and ornament were highly calculated.

■ the influence of palladio

It is surprising that Andrea Palladio had very little influence during his lifetime, even over the architecture in Italy, although his publications of the principles of Vitruvius were certainly well known. Indeed, it was Palladio's pupil and assistant Vincenzo Scamozzi, the author of a long treatise on architecture, who effectively brought Palladio's work to the notice of architects in other parts of Europe (particularly Holland and Germany).

But it was Inigo Jones, a visitor to Rome in the winter of 1613, who readily embraced Palladio's ideas and was influential enough in his own country – England – to popularize them. Nevertheless it was another century before the great revival of Palladio's designs was to take place, when between 1720 and 1760 Palladianism was the dominant architectural style in Britain.

ABOVE Palazzo Chiericati, Vicenza, Italy (Palladio, started 1550). The grandest town residence by Palladio. Originally on the outskirts of Vicenza, it is now surrounded by the town. The double loggia façade must have impressed Inigo Jones, for it is clearly the inspiration for the Queen's House at Greenwich. However, the façade is inside-out with a recessed portico centrally at first-floor level.

LEFT Teatro Olympico, Vicenza, Italy (Palladio, 1580). This theatre has a permanent stage set with a street scene in false perspective, so that in reality it is only a matter of a metre of so in depth. It is based on early Roman models. The sculpture and detailing are magnificent.

▶ bramante

Donato Bramante is often ranked with Raphael and Michelangelo as one of those who represent the full flowering of the Renaissance in Italy. He too started as a painter, but it is for his architectural prowess and influence that he remains famous today.

He was born Donato d'Angelo near Urbino, and may have been a distant relation of Raphael. At Urbino as a child and young man he came under the benign influence of the Renaissance theorist Alberti and the artist Piero della Francesca. He earned his living as a painter, working, for instance, on the frescoes at the Palazzo del Podestà in Bergamo. But at the age of 36 he left for Milan and restricted himself to the study and practice of architecture.

In Milan he absorbed much of the architectural style of Leonardo da Vinci (who became his friend) and studied the classical forms used by Brunelleschi. Some of these ideas are apparent in his major commissions in the city, the church of Sta Maria presso San Satiro and parts of Sta Maria delle Grazie.

As a result of invasion by French forces, Bramante left Milan for Rome in 1499. There he found many more examples of classical art to study and learn from, and his architectural style thereupon changed accordingly. From about 1503 Bramante worked on a highly prestigious commission: designs for the rebuilding of St Peter's for Pope Julius II. Construction work actually began in 1506. Bramante died, however, in 1514 before the work had got very far, and his designs were in any case radically altered by later architects, notably Michelangelo. But surviving works by Bramante in Rome include the Tempietto at San Pietro in Montorio, a tiny church that fulfils in miniature many of the design ideas Bramante intended for the new St Peter's, and several lesser buildings in the Vatican.

Bramante's main influence was perhaps in the classical ideals and the Renaissance principles of harmony and unity that he passed on to the many pupils he taught in Rome. In Raphael's fresco *The School of Athens* Bramante is shown as Euclid.

BELOW Certosa, Pavia, Italy (1473). A façade added to an earlier Gothic church, though any traces of the original have been adapted or concealed by the new architecture. It is an extraordinary achievement, carried out entirely in different marbles and decorated by the greatest sculptors of the day.

RIGHT San Biagio, Montepulciano, Italy (1519–26). Antonio da Sangallo, the elder (1455–1534). This church has an interesting and ingenious design, in which a square bell tower fits snugly into one of the recesses left by the Greek cross plan. To complete the composition, a Bramante-like dome sits high over the crossing. The actual façade is remarkably restrained, giving the pedimented door and window openings greater vitality.

LEFT Palazzo Massimi, Rome (Peruzzi, 1535). A pupil of Bramante's, he designed this small palace on a difficult curved site on a busy Roman street. The treatment of this facade is faultless: an imposing ground floor of columns supporting a heavy cornice, with a floor above (piano nobile) of tall windows linked by blank balconies. The top two storeys have simple framed windows set into deeply cut formal stonework. The wide eaves above accentuate the curving shadows cast on the rounded façade.

BELOW Santa Maria della Consolazione, Todi, Italy (1508). Cola da Caprarola (dates unknown). This unusual church is based on the old Byzantine Greek cross plan, but unlike San Marco in Venice, for example, it is very tall and tightly integrated. Here is the archetypal Renaissance dome, supported on a high drum, which was to be repeated all over Europe in the following centuries.

▶ the sangallo family

The Sangallo family provided several talented architects in Florence and Rome during the later 15th century and the early 16th century.

Giuliano de Sangallo, who was born in around 1445, was an architect employed by the de' Medici family, rulers of Florence. He designed and built a villa at Poggio a Caiano for them in 1485. Perhaps his major triumph was the church of the Madonna delle Carceri in Prato, of roughly the same date. Designed in the shape of a Greek cross, the church shows the strong influence of Brunelleschi's ideas on harmony and unity of composition. Giuliano was a contemporary of Bramante and became acquainted with him during visits to Rome; it may have been through this contact that Giuliano's newphew Antonio the Younger was sent later to Rome to study under Bramante. Towards the end of his life Giuliano carried out important commissions on the façade of San Lorenzo in Florence. He died in 1516.

Antonio da Sangallo (the Elder) was Giuliano's brother, possibly ten years younger. He too came under the influence of Bramante and because of it eventually became a more powerful designer than Giuliano. His major work is the church of San Biagio in Montepulciano. He died in 1534.

Antonio Picconi da Sangallo (the Younger) was the nephew of Giuliano and Antonio the Elder, and was born in 1483. A pupil of Bramante in Rome, from whom he gained an enthusiasm for the arts of classical Rome that he retained all his life, he later became the foremost Italian architect of his day, succeeding Raphael as the architect on the ongoing construction of St Peter's. Other great patrons of his included the Farnese family for whom he designed the Farnese Palace in Rome (begun in 1518), a fortified palace at Caprarola, and several other buildings. His commissions also involved work as a military engineer and city planner. He died in 1546.

■ tudor times and after in england

The influx of foreign artists and craftsmen to the court of Henry VIII, introducing the ideas of the Renaissance, prompted a reaction to elaborate brick detailing. The large houses built during the reigns of Elizabeth I and James I show a more restrained handling of the material. There is a change in the relationship between solid and void, as windows became larger, and the buildings take on the character of country houses rather than fortified dwellings.

Hatfield House (1607–11) is a good example of this change of emphasis. The openings are framed in stone and the brickwork serves merely to provide a continuous plane surface, against which the drama of the openings is contrasted. The quoins (angles at the corners) are formed in stone, which emphasizes the planar quality of the brickwork; instead of there being a continuous undulating surface able to accommodate turrets and towers, the brickwork is treated as a series of panels which meet with precision and control.

If Hatfield House anticipates the severely classical treatment of the Banqueting House (Inigo Jones, 1619–21), there was also a secondary line of development in brick construction which culminated in the wealth of late Stuart and early Georgian houses. Since Tudor times, the highest skills of the brickmaker and bricklayer had been exercised in the production of moulded and carved brickwork. These skills were reinforced by the arrival of immigrants from Flanders and the Netherlands, who introduced the technique of gauged brickwork. This involved making very soft bricks which could be cut with a saw and then rubbed to a precise, gauged shape. Since it was possible to achieve a high degree of accuracy, gauged brickwork required very fine joints. The earliest example of gauged brickwork is at the Dutch House, Kew (1631). The wall is dissolved in a series of finely moulded and carved details, surmounted with curved gables which finish in curved or triangular pediments. Although the design is robust, the building displays an enthusiasm for using brick as structure and decoration.

Brick served the Tudor court and the Elizabethan gentry, but in early Georgian times it became the preserve of middle class merchants and professional men. High fashion and style were the concern of those who had travelled in Italy, while a comfortable formality was the preoccupation of the emerging middle-class. Skilled craftsmanship was expected from the builders who followed their pattern books and faithfully reproduced a wide range of details. Gauged brickwork in arches and even, in exceptional circumstances, on the whole front elevation; recessed panels with intricate patterns; raised decoration, cornices, string-courses; in situ carving and moulded brickwork – the whole range of the bricklayer's art was employed and can still be seen today forming the nucleus of many English country towns.

TOP Wollaton Hall, Nottinghamshire, England (1580–88). Built by Robert Smythson (c 1536–1614), the castle has a fairytale shape. Its design was revolutionary for the Elizabethan times. The corner towers were placed symmetrically around the massive central Great Hall.

ABOVE Banqueting House, Whitehall, London (1619). Inigo Jones (1573–1652). After studying the buildings of Palladio in Italy, Jones returned home where he revolutionized English architecture. The severely classical but accomplished banqueting chamber was to have been but a tiny part of a gigantic Palace of Whitehall, which, if it had been completed, would have been among the largest in Europe.

▶ inigo jones

Little is known about Inigo Jones before he reached the age of 30 in 1603. By that time, however, he was an accomplished draughtsman and stage designer, and had visited Italy where the effects of the Renaissance were in full exhibition in all the arts. Shortly afterwards he took up a position in the royal court, for decades thereafter designing and producing masques for the sovereign's entertainment.

In 1613 he travelled with the Earl of Arundel to Germany and to Italy, spending the whole of the winter period in Rome. It was on this trip that Jones absorbed the works of Palladio, an architect whose neo-classical principles he later introduced and popularized in England.

From 1615 to 1644, Jones's main occupation was the design or alteration of royal houses, generally in the style of Palladio. Few survive unchanged today, although his work remains very much visible in the Queen's House at Greenwich, the Banqueting House in Whitehall and the Queen's Chapel at St James's Palace. Jones was also responsible for introducing the idea of a public square to London.

He died in London in 1652.

LEFT Audley End, Essex, England (1603–1616). The huge mullioned windows, particularly on the first floor, are really Perpendicular in spirit. Classical details are restricted to unambitious mouldings on the ground floor.

■ the renaissance elsewhere in europe

▶ cornelis floris

The major influence on the life of Cornelis Floris — born Cornelis de Vriendt in Antwerp, Belgium, in 1514 — was the trip he took with his younger brother Frans to Rome in the early 1540s. There the two young men studied the art of antiquity while at the same time absorbing the tenets of the Renaissance masters of the day, and both returned home to Belgium with minds and notebooks full of impressions.

Both Cornelis and Frans rapidly established their own workshops in Antwerp, Cornelis as an architect and sculptor, and Frans as a painter. The brothers were remarkably successful, although Frans's extravagant way of life meant that despite his acknowledged genius and the efficient running of his workshop he was forever out of funds and deeply in debt.

Cornelis is celebrated for his Antwerp Town Hall which, with its amalgamation of a Gothic gable front and a Florentine palace façade, became the model for many other town halls in Flanders and the Netherlands. The town hall was completed in 1565, and has been described as the finest and most influential building of the 16th century in the Low Countries.

Other major commissions were for the tombs of the Danish kings Frederick I at Schleswig in Germany and Christian II at Roskilde in Denmark, and for the choir screen of the cathedral at Tournai in Belgium. Cornelis's architectural style — a "somewhat severe Renaissance style" according to one authoritative commentator — was thus well known in a number of countries of northern Europe, and in this way Cornelis helped to spread the new principles and methods of the Renaissance further abroad.

Cornelis died in 1575, five years after his brother Frans.

BELOW Hôtel de Ville, Antwerp, Belgium (1560–65). (Cornelis Floris, 1514–75). An early Renaissance building of great distinction and good proportions. The stepped central gable is distinctly Flemish. The top storey, which forms an open gallery under the subtly curved roof, is an original and felicitous invention. The building was destroyed in 1576 and immediately rebuilt.

BELOW RIGHT Escorial, Madrid (1562–84). Juan de Herrera (1530–97). A distant view of the great lonely palace and monastery built for Philip II outside Madrid. The plan is a gigantic rectangle, divided into courtyards with a large central church.

► the style of juan de herrera

Juan de Herrera has been described as the greatest Spanish architect of the 16th century. The Herreran style named after him certainly came about through his mediumship although he was not totally responsible for all the aspects pertaining to it. The style is as much a product of the time, place and patronage involved in the construction of a single building — the Escorial, a palace-monastery just outside Madrid — as it is of the design skill of one man.

That the style is renowned as cold and austere owes much to the character of the patron for whom the Escorial was built: the melancholic, religious fanatic King Philip II (sometime husband of Mary Tudor, Queen of England). The initial plan — a vast rectangular building, with a large church at its centre — was drawn up by Juan Bautista de Toledo. The overall architectural style and the execution of the actual construction was at the hand of Herrera, Toledo's assistant and successor — after King Philip had overseen the designs and removed anything ornamental or ostentatious.

The result is severe, plain exterior walls with row upon row of unadorned windows emphasizing an evident conventual character; inside the strict simplicity is repeated in the total absence of decorative elements. Yet there are aspects of the Renaissance: Doric columns support the classic triangular pediment over the central portal's exterior, and there are further Doric columns inside. The Doric order is the least ornamented of the three classic orders of antiquity.

The Escorial, with its impressive mass and overall dimensions, is said to have an additional forbidding quality unmatched by any other building.

This, then, is the Herreran style, but Juan de Herrera went on to design other buildings, among them the cathedral at Valladolid (begun 1585) and the Lonja court at Seville (completed in 1599).

Herrera died in 1597, nearing the age of 70

TOP Grote Markt, Antwerp, Belgium (c 1579). Stepped gables like these were one of the happiest contributions of Dutch and Flemish architecture. The tall windows, huge in proportion to their wall surface, are another characteristic of the period.

ABOVE Palais de Justice, Liège, Belgium (1526). Because of its geographical position, Belgium was influenced by both French and German neighbours. The French influence here is shown by the roof and semicircular pediment, while the minute clock tower is Flemish.

history and the new forms

As the Renaissance was founded in fifteenth-century Florence, so its continuation through Mannerism to Baroque was a Roman inspiration. The term Baroque has come to be attached to architecture (and more recently, to music), but its origins are really much deeper, profoundly associated with religion, painting and literature.

The Counter Reformation in the late sixteenth century made Rome an uncomfortable place in which to live. Powered by the ascetic founder of the Jesuits, St Ignatius Loyola, the movement had introduced the purging of heretics and with this the Inquisition. Visitors from more easy-going republics like Venice found Rome a joyless city. Masquerades and pageants declined, or were forbidden. Michelangelo, himself an ascetic, offered his services to design the new church of the Gesù for nothing. His later

works are suffused with feelings of disquiet, ambiguity and barely contained violence. Nudity in painting, except for impeccably religious purposes, gave way to figures clad in draperies which were voluminous and exaggerated, full of restless movement. Three-dimensional representation was heightened by the use of theatrical lighting – "chiaroscuro" (light and dark), the new and dramatic technique in painting characteristic of painters such as Caravaggio and Tintoretto.

The new movement infected architecture. The fluent Mannerism of Giulio Romano (1492–1546) gave way to the expressionism of Bernini and Borromini. Elements of cruelty, sexual repression and violence found outlets in the new art and suited exactly the dramatic evangelism of the Jesuits. Perhaps for this reason the Baroque has always been unpopular in the Protestant north. The great English Victorian art critic, John Ruskin, termed it the "Grotesque

ABOVE Claude Nicolas Ledoux (1736–1806). While the spirit of the Baroque is antagonistic to strict classicism, Classical elements form the basis of the style. Ledoux's evocation of Italianate Classicism is here seen modified by a romantic spirit. His projects are part of the Baroque ethos. In 1775 he was invited to provide buildings surrounding a saltworks at Chaux in eastern France, a project never fully carried out. The theatrical entrance portico places strictly classical columns and entablature against freely carved rocks.

Renaissance", recoiling in distaste when he found examples of it shoulder to shoulder with the early churches and palaces of his beloved Venice. Interestingly enough this lack of sympathy for the style in architecture did not extend to painters like his beloved Tintoretto, a Baroque painter of genius above all others.

Other factors besides religion and painting refuelled the new style. The Renaissance discovery of the laws of perspective had led to a revolution in three-dimensional representation. Draperies became both more naturalistic and exaggerated: similarly in architecture the old forms of square, rectangle, circle and dome were found to be worked out. New forms were sought, and among these the oval became predominant, because while geometrical, it could nevertheless be extended or squeezed at will. On plan it could be crossed or integrated with other ovals, giving rise to exotic serpentine shapes, themselves echoed by oval arches, domes and cupolas above. This spatial and restless architecture became the perfect acoustic envelope for the new music. The great church services and masses of Monteverdi and Vivaldi rang out among its curved walls and domes. Religion regained, for a time, something of the theatrical wonder of the medieval past, to which virtuosity, even if highly artificial, added new dimensions of space and theatre to further its ends.

The seventeenth century was also an age of intense scientific discovery and curiosity and the effect this had on the arts and religion was significant. Galileo and Copernicus had shifted the Earth away from its previous position as centre of the Universe to a humbler status as just one heavenly body among countless others. The new concept of infinity itself was as exciting and disquieting to the artist as it was to the clergy. In this light, the Baroque should be seen as a second phase to the Renaissance, not as a decline or debasement of a pure original. It was an architecture exploring the mystery of space, of worlds beyond the known world, beyond too, the simple philosophical humanism of the preceding century.

ABOVE CENTRE Chiswick House, London (1726). Lord Burlington (1694–1753) and William Kent (1685–1748). The English Palladian villa. With the death of the great Baroque architects, Palladianism became re-established as the predominant English style. Kent had been sent to Italy to record buildings and on his return collaborated with his patron. Lord Burlington, a talented amateur, on this reconstruction of Palladio's Villa Rotonda into a northern and perhaps less appropriate climate.

ABOVE Stourhead, Wiltshire, England (1722). Colen Campbell (1673–1729). If one detaches the later wings, the essentially Palladian villa is revealed. Campbell was one of the most versatile early Georgian architects, devoted to the works of Palladio and Inigo Jones.

RIGHT Ecstasy of St Teresa, Sta Maria della Vittoria, Rome (Bernini, 1642–52). The dramatic presentation embodies the essence of the Baroque and its vital link between sculpture and architecture. Never before had religious subjects been treated with such theatrical and expressionist realism.

■ the baroque in rome

The two dominating figures of Roman Baroque are almost exact contemporaries and rivals. Gianlorenzo Bernini (1598–1680) was a brilliant sculptor who turned to architecture. His junior by a year, Francesco Borromini (1599–1667), started as an apprentice sculptor but became an architect. The technical virtuosity of Bernini is extraordinary. Nothing shows this better than his sculpture of *Apollo and Daphne*. All is movement and its translation into white marble is consummate. It is as far from the monumental Classicism of Michelangelo's statues as the new architecture of Borromini was from that of Bramante or Alberti.

Such pagan triumphs as Apollo and Daphne were tolerated by the Church but Bernini's religious sculpture was equally theatrical. His most celebrated work in this genre is the amazing *Ecstasy of St Teresa* in a side chapel of Sta Maria della Vittoria in Rome. The semi-reclining figure of the saint, voluminously draped, is lying with her eyes closed in ecstasy. There is an erotic ambiguity to the pose; the figure of the smiling angel does nothing to relieve the emotionally loaded tableau. The Roman family standing to one side, as if at the theatre, implies that the agony was laid on for their entertainment. The whole effect is subtly emphasized by the carefully contrived use of lighting from above, the light emanating from a source that is not revealed: a favourite trick of Bernini's.

▶ bernini

Giovanni Lorenzo Bernini was probably the greatest sculptor of the 17th century, but was also a leading architect (and a dramatist, stage designer and painter). In sculpture he alone was virtually responsible for the creation of what came to be called the Baroque style.

Born in Naples in December 1598, he was the son of a Florentine sculptor then based mostly in Rome. He proved himself to be something of a child prodigy, and established himself as an independent sculptor at an unusually early age. He produced highly artistic works in his own style, although the work is of an evidently immature hand. By the age of 19 he was already producing works of sculpture for Cardinal Maffeo Barberini. The cardinal later became Pope Urban VIII and Bernini's most consistent patron, particularly in the commissioning of architectural designs.

In the meantime he executed sculptural commissions for the equally prestigious papal family, the Borghese family, and several portrait busts of other ecclesiastical notables. The style of these was distinctly different from the Mannerism of the time.

Bernini's first architectural commission was the redesigning of the church of Sta Bibiana, although his second became far more famous: the ornate baldacchino over the tomb of St Peter in St Peter's. The twisted columns at each corner relate to columns used in early Christian times for altar screens, and the metallic drapes echo the canopies held over persons and sites of particular significance. The entire monument is also covered with emblems of the Barberini family: bees, suns, and laurel shoots.

Bernini also designed much of the interior of St Peter's, all of it in a lively and personal style. Further busts of Roman ecclesiasts followed, then commissions for tombs and fountains and chapels, all including grand statuary and intricate ornament. The fountains are possibly his most memorable contributions to the urban Roman scene, combining both sculpture and architecture. The chapels generally provided a similar combination, with some of the statuary subtly emphasized by exotic lighting effects from hidden sources. Probably the greatest example of this is the statue of St Teresa in the Cornaro Chapel in Sta Maria della Vittoria.

He was extremely active into his old age: he produced the Altieri Chapel in San Francesco a Ripa, which is up to his best standards, at the age of 75 – but by then he had seen styles of design begin to change again. He died in 1680, aged 81.

TOP The Colonnade, St Peter's, Rome (Bernini, 1656–67). The sculptor-architect Bernini laid out a huge oval piazza in front of the cathedral, flanked by colossal colonnades with double columns each side. The aim, brilliantly realized, was to embrace pilgrims within the two arms of the great mother church, which lay at the focus of the composition.

ABOVE This view of St Peter's interior shows Bernini's gilt *cathedra Petri* topped by a sunburst window. The giant Corinthian order pilasters lend background monumentality.

ABOVE San Andrea delle Fratte, Rome (1653). Borromini was commissioned to complete the interior of this church, the nave of which had already been started.

LEFT San Carlo alle Quatro Fontane, Rome (Borromini, 1665). A small masterpiece of Roman High Baroque. Squeezed into a tiny site at the corner of a crowded square, this extraordinary serpentine façade conceals an interior of equally sinuous forms and spatial dexterity.

▶ borromini

Francesco Borromini is often cited as a great rival of Bernini – but the suggestion is slightly misleading. Although they were certainly contemporaries, Bernini was additionally a great sculptor, which Borromini was not. In addition they influenced each other considerably whereas rivals try to differ from each other, not imitate. Above all, Borromini was at one stage Bernini's assistant, organizing the execution of Bernini's designs. To a great extent, Borromini was as brilliantly innovative in architecture as Bernini was in sculpture, and this difference was noted at the time. The one-time assistant may finally have rivalled the one-time master – but only in eminence.

Borromini was born in 1599 (just over 9 months later than Bernini) in northern Italy. Initially, between the ages of 9 and 14, he was trained as a stone mason in Milan, before going to Rome to work under the direction of the architect Carlo Maderno at St Peter's. Fifteen years later he had progressed to the position of Bernini's assistant in the latter's commissions at the Palazzo Barberini as well as at St Peter's. Borromini was in charge of the execution of Bernini's great altar canopy in St Peter's.

He then began to take on independent commissions, the first of which was the design of the small church and cloister of San Carlo alle Quattro Fontane in Rome. Work began in 1633 and continued for 10 years. He was to add a façade to the church some 20 years later still. The outline of the church was formed by intersecting ovals, resulting in an undulating or serpentine interior wall surface that Borromini thereafter favoured all his life. The church even had an oval-shaped dome. Overall, the effect was dynamic.

In contrast the church of Sant' Ivo della Sapienza was designed in the shape of a six-pointed star; a complex dome rose from the centre. The design dated from 1642. Earlier Borromini was responsible for the Oratorio di San Filippo Neri (1637) and a colonnade added to the Palazzo Spada (1632); later he refurbished the interior of San Giovanni in Laterano (1646) and designed the church of Sant' Agnese in the Piazza Navona (1653).

Although Borromini used the classical components of architecture, he is considered to have done so in a freer fashion than anyone of the previous century or of his own day. He featured apparently disparate elements while still emphasizing the overall unity of composition.

He died in Rome in August 1667.

LEFT Sant' Ivo della Sapienza, Rome (Borromini, 1642–60). The amazing spiral finial to the lantern which completes the dome of the star-shaped church of the University of Rome. The strange juxtaposition of forms shows Borromini exercising his unrestrained sculptural expressionism.

ABOVE Il Gesù, Rome (1568–75). Giacomo Vignola (1507–73). Façade by Giacomo della Porta (c 1537–1602). The classical good manners of the front of the Gesù, with its side scrolls, conceals a more obviously Baroque interior. The style was closely connected with the new Jesuitical movement and this church was designed for the large following which the new order attracted.

Inside, the church shows the early Baroque experiments with space and movement, combined with eighteenth-century marble wall coverings. Preaching was an important part of the new form of service and Vignola provided an ample nave and well-lit crossing for the congregation. The church is transitional between Mannerism and High Baroque.

◼ borromini and the spread of baroque

Borromini dealt in different forms. A more private and tortured personality than his rival (he was to kill himself after a period of insanity), his art was abstract, concentrated and deeply personal. Later, he might have been called an architectural Expressionist, and certainly nothing like his manipulation of form had been seen before, definitely not in Europe. Indeed some of his forms, like the strange spiral finial to the church of Sant' Ivo (page 72), seem to owe their inspiration to the ancient architecture of Syria or to the then unknown Far East.

After Borromini, Baroque travelled north, first to Piedmont, then across the Alps to Austria, Germany and central Europe. It also followed the Catholic trail to Spain and Portugal and from there, in due course, to South America. In other countries it withered or was modified, as in France and England. The Château of Vaux Le Vicompte by Le Vau, south of Paris, is Baroque in its great, oval-domed salon, yet it is clearly restrained by an earlier Classicism. Likewise the Baroque architects of England, Christopher Wren (1632–1723), James Gibbs (1682–1754) and Thomas Archer (1668–1743) never approached the organic suppleness or extremism of a Borromini. Only in the monumental and highly sculptural works of John Vanbrugh (1664–1726) and Nicholas Hawksmoor (1661–1736) are some of the uneasy and equivocal qualities of their Italian inspiration manifested. Seaton Delaval by Vanbrugh in Northumberland, and Christchurch, Spitalfields in London by Hawksmoor, both display an unnerving remoteness foreign to the gentler Palladianism of their contemporaries.

After Borromini, it might be seen that nothing further could possibly be accomplished in this direction. Curiously enough the final phase of Baroque, the rococo, was triggered by interior decoration in France. The term Baroque derived from an Italian word meaning flawed pearl, and Rococo derived from the French *rocaille,* the sea rocks and shells from which a new form of ornament was introduced. It suited the French style and its fantastic forms, free and wholly decorative, came in time to modify and lighten the Baroque superstructure itself. Its greatest genius was shown in the churches of southern Germany and Bavaria. In England it was almost entirely an indoor art, carried out in stucco applications to walls and ceilings.

As Baroque had been a reaction to Vitruvian discipline, so it too eventually gave way to a return to earlier Classicism, based on recent archaeological discoveries in Greece and Italy. It was never an easy art to master. In the hands of Borromini or Vanbrugh it is ravishing: in lesser hands it falls too easily into licence and superficial vulgarity. Perhaps of all architectural styles, it is for the toughest and most accomplished talents only.

ABOVE Panthéon, Paris (1757–80). Jacques Soufflot (1713–80). A simple Greek cross church entered under a giant Corinthian order portico. This neo-Classical building bears comparison with St Paul's in London, particularly with Wren's early but rejected model, based on a similar plan. The interior is equally cool and assured, employing modulations of detached columns and pilasters.

ABOVE RIGHT The magnificence at Versailles continued into the garden with vast formal layouts by the landscape architect André le Nôtre (1613–1700). These were based on complex axial avenues which gave the spectator glimpses of lake, fountains and sculptures. The palace on this elevation is, on account of its sheer size, impressive, but the unrelieved roofline makes for monotony.

RIGHT The Palace of Versailles, France. (Le Vau, 1669–1674). Louis XIV's famous palace complex is built around an older hunting palace. The entrance façade is one of the grandest in Europe. The absence of planting and the giant cobbles underfoot add to the brutal approach to this magnificent symbol of France's age of power and influence.

▶ ledoux

Claude Nicolas Ledoux was something of an eccentric among architects of the 18th century. Although in general he obeyed the tenets of the Baroque and neo-Classical styles of his age, he nevertheless also produced designs for houses in the shapes of globes, cylinders and pyramids that have no parallel in the history of architecture. These were evident attempts to break away from traditionalism, from styles that had in effect been popular for more than a century. Not until modern times have such designs received genuine interest. To some extent this is due to the fact that the materials with which to execute such designs are only now readily available.

Ledoux was born in 1736 at Dormans-sur-Marne, France. He sprang to fame through his designs for the houses of several aristocrats including Madame du Barry (last mistress of Louis XV). Between 1775 and 1779 he was responsible for the construction of the factory buildings and the houses of the workers at the royal saltworks at Arc-et-Senans in Franche-Comté. In roughly the same period he designed the theatre in Besançon. Four of the tollhouses he built in Paris remain to this day.

Because of his connections with aristocrats, it was not surprising that in 1793, towards the middle of the French Revolution, he was for a time imprisoned as a suspected royalist. Once free, however, he absorbed himself solely in writing his treatise on architecture — published in 1804 under the title *L'architecture* — in which he outlined the shape of buildings to come (as described initially above). He regarded such forms as ideals of the constructive art.

He died in Paris in November 1806.

BELOW The Royal Saltworks, Arc-et-Senans, France (Ledoux, 1775). The Director's Stables (**BOTTOM**) is more like a temple; its rusticated façade and bold geometrical openings elevating it above the merely practical. Likewise, the Director's own house (**BELOW**) is an exercise in the grandiose, yet rescued from pretentiousness by the force of its architectural coherence.

▶ fischer von erlach

Johann Bernhard Fischer von Erlach is said to have been the founder and chief exponent of the Baroque arts in Austria. He was both a sculptor and an architect, and was born near Graz in July 1656.

His architectural training was at the workshop of Giovanni Lorenzo Bernini, the greatest sculptor of the age, in Rome. It was there he learned the elements of architecture, and how to combine architecture and sculpture successfully.

After this basic grounding, Fischer von Erlach returned to Austria. Inevitably, he had progressed beyond any potential artistic rival. He rapidly became the official court architect (to no fewer than three emperors in succession), and his advice and work were constantly sought by the aristocracy, including in particular the influential archbishop of Salzburg.

Yet despite Bernini's tutelage, Fischer Von Erlach had strong ideas of his own on the subject of ideal forms of architecture — ideas that might not have corresponded with Bernini's. For instance, he was prepared to mix styles. His motifs were found not just in the Classical buildings of ancient Rome and in the Renaissance forms derived from them, but also in the Italian Baroque, the French Rococo, and even in versions exhibited in contemporary English architecture. This was in an attempt to find a solution to each problem that was not necessarily unique, but that expressed in totality all the features of the actual purpose of each building. To fulfil his concept of glorifying the patron saint of a building, Fischer von Erlach might "borrow" features from various sources. The combination of these features, each complete in themselves, would display all the qualities associated with the saint that adherents might find useful in their devotions. The theory is analogous to the philosophy of Gottfried Leibniz, a famous contemporary of Fischer's, whose metaphysical expositions saw divine harmony in systems of interrelated units.

Fischer designed many important buildings in Vienna, including the Schönbrunn Palace and several other imperial residences. In Salzburg he was responsible for Holy Trinity and University churches and the archbishop's house. He also wrote an important history of architecture: *Entwurff einer historischen Architectur,* published in 1721.

He died in Vienna in April 1723.

ABOVE LEFT Schönbrunn Palace, Vienna, Austria (1695–1750). Fischer von Erlach (1656–1723). Designed as a rival to Versailles. The architecture is much lighter, however, and the use of pale, warm colours – cream, yellow with white and gold – sets it firmly in Central Europe. Inside, the decorations are Rococo. The flowing profusion of forms and exaggerated perspective are characteristic.

TOP LEFT Amalienburg Palace, Munich, Germany (1734). Francois Cuvilliés (1695–1768). The French appearance of this building in the grounds of the Nymphenburg Palace is no accident as it was designed by Cuvilliés, a court dwarf who was found to have architectural gifts and was sent to study in Paris. On his return he created, among other works, this charming little summer pavilion.

▶ von hildebrandt

Born of German parents in Genoa, Italy, in November 1668, Johann Lucas von Hildebrandt was actually trained in Rome under the direction of Carlo Fontana and Colonel Ceruti as an architect, town planner and military engineer. And it was mainly as a military engineer that he began his career, participating with the Imperial Army in three campaigns in Piedmont under Prince Eugene of Savoy. However, he then moved to Vienna and at the age of 31 became engineer to the Austrian royal court. Fischer von Erlach influenced his ideas there, although the older man had already passed the peak of his popularity. When Fischer died in 1723, Hildebrandt in turn became the leading royal architect.

In some respects, the work of Hildebrandt resembles Fischer's — he too preferred to put together a synthesis of different architectural styles from previous ages in order to reflect a theme in a building more thoroughly. However, his strength lay more in the ornamentation of buildings than in the overall plan, and his introduction of new motifs into Austrian Baroque architecture — using specific decorative features for specific types of building — meant that the buildings constructed were at first easily recognized (once the types became known) and afterwards readily imitated. Few of his designs are in any way unique, therefore; his principles and ideas spread rapidly throughout the Habsburg empire, to southern and western Germany, and even to nearby Balkan states. In this way Hildebrandt could be said to have been far more influential to the dissemination of Austrian Baroque architectural style than even Fischer von Erlach.

In Vienna, major works by Hildebrandt still standing include the summer residence of Prince Eugene, the Starhemberg garden palace, the Austrian Chancellery and Göttweig monastery; he also rebuilt the Mirabell Palace in Salzburg and redesigned Ràckeve Castle near Budapest. But he was also responsible for a multitude of parish churches, villas, town houses and garden pavilions for the Austrian bourgeoisie.

Hildebrandt died in Vienna in November 1745.

ABOVE AND BELOW RIGHT
Nymphenburg Palace, Munich, Germany (1717–23). Built in the Bavarian Court style, the outside is formal, almost severe. By contrast, the interior is highly decorated, with flowery plaster relief, gilded or silvered and set against white and coloured backgrounds. In imitation of Versailles, four pavilions were added, linked by galleries.

ABOVE The Zwinger, Dresden, Germany (1711–22). M. D. Pöppelmann (1622–1736). Built as a kind of large playhouse and pleasure gardens for Augustus of Saxony; it fronts a huge open square in the centre of Dresden. Destroyed in the Second World War, it has since been restored.

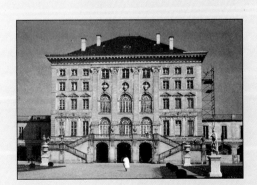

▶ wren

Sir Christopher Wren was born the son of a clergyman in Wiltshire, England, in October 1632. Educated at Westminster School until the age of 14, he attended Oxford University to pursue scientific studies. There he was elected a fellow of All Souls College in the same year that he attained his master's degree. It was as professor of astronomy that he moved to Gresham College, London, then back to Oxford in 1661. Wren was a co-founder of the Royal Society together with a slightly younger Sir Isaac Newton.

Gradually, however, architecture began to dominate all other interests. His first architectural commissions were to design the chapel of Pembroke College, Cambridge (for his uncle, Bishop Matthew Wren) and the hall "theatre" at Oxford. It was at about this time – 1665 – that Wren travelled to France where, in Paris, he met the great Bernini (then aged 66) and marvelled at the Rococo buildings of King Louis XIV's royal establishment.

Shortly after his return to England, the Great Fire of London made the reconstruction of much of the city an urgent necessity. Wren presented a complete plan which, although it was not accepted, ensured him an influential seat on the commission for rebuilding.

Besides St Paul's cathedral, more than 50 other London churches had to be designed and built anew. Religious traditions and contemporary fashions were important, but Wren nonetheless managed to create a great variety of types of building, many of which also incorporated aspects of the style of Inigo Jones (who had died nearly 20 years earlier). Particularly noteworthy are Wren's elaborate spires and the dome of the church of St Stephen, Walbrook.

The designing of the new St Paul's presented many problems. Wren was determined that the building should equal the finest in contemporary Italy or France, whereas the incumbent clergy yearned for something more traditional, reminiscent of the medieval, and of the capital's primary church. He was obliged to produce design after design. The design that was finally accepted underwent substantial changes during the actual construction. The eventual triple dome – the epitome of Baroque – has been described as "structurally and aesthetically a remarkable achievement", and even today, dwarfed by surrounding high-rise blocks, it dominates the skyline.

Retaining his position on the commission for rebuilding, Wren continued to provide buildings for the city of London and its surrounds for years afterwards. It was only after political intrigues intervened in 1718 (when Wren was 85) that he was finally dismissed from his post. He died five years later, and was interred in St Paul's.

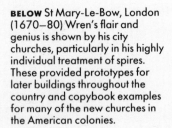

BELOW St Mary-Le-Bow, London (1670–80) Wren's flair and genius is shown by his city churches, particularly in his highly individual treatment of spires. These provided prototypes for later buildings throughout the country and copybook examples for many of the new churches in the American colonies.

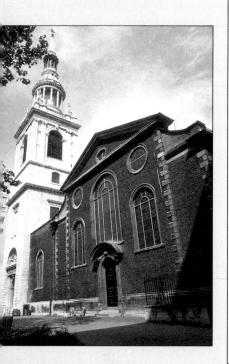

ABOVE Christchurch, Spitalfields, London (1723–39). Hawksmoor, for many years an assistant to Wren and Clerk of Works at St Paul's, was a more sombre and deliberate architect than his tutor. This church is assembled like some ancient tomb, its tower terminating in an anachronistic but magnificent Gothic steeple. It is one of the most extraordinary buildings of its time.

▶ vanbrugh

Sir John Vanbrugh is probably better known today as one of the great writers of Restoration comedy plays, yet he has been described as "a creator of the English Baroque style in architecture".

In fact, in 1699 at the age of 35 and already a seasoned playwright, Vanbrugh designed Castle Howard in Yorkshire, England. He was probably entirely untrained, and he quite definitely relied on professional help (notably from Christopher Wren's clerk, Nicholas Hawksmoor). However the result was inspirational, essentially combining numbers of Classical elements with space and light, and arranging the building within an unusually picturesque setting. His emphasis on environmental beauty later led to a distinctive style of English garden half way to the naturalism of William Kent.

Other major architectural commissions were Kimbolton Castle, Claremont (in Surrey), Kings Weston (Gloucestershire) and, particularly, Woodstock (Oxfordshire). Blenheim Palace at Woodstock was the nation's gift to the soldier-hero Duke of Marlborough, intended to be – as it became – the architectural gem of the reign of Queen Anne. Hawksmoor was again vital in partnership, and the result is magnificent.

A man of an extraordinary double life, Vanbrugh died in 1726 in London.

TOP RIGHT Radcliffe Camera, Oxford, England (1737–49). Gibbs was unusual among English architects in having studied abroad; he worked in Rome in the studio of Carlo Fontana. Setting up in practice in England, his architecture reflects his attempt to resolve his Mannerist background with contemporary English Palladianism. The circular plan of this domed library perfectly fits its courtyard site; a building of which his tutor would surely have approved.

RIGHT Blenheim Palace, Oxfordshire, England (Vanbrugh, 1705–24). Built by the state for the Duke of Marlborough in recognition of his military achievements. Vanbrugh is an attractive figure in English architecture, equally or more famous as a dramatist. Some of this sense of theatre can be seen in his buildings, tempered by the professionalism of his collaborator, Hawksmoor, whose hand can be seen in many of the details.

RIGHT Castle Howard, Yorkshire, England (Vanbrugh, 1699–1712). The greatest of this architect's country houses, the nearest equivalent in English terms to the French château or Italian palazzo. The great entrance lies under the central dome and rises the full height of the building, flanked by staircases. Vanbrugh was again assisted by Hawksmoor, but the individual character of the playwright-architect seems to dominate.

LEFT, RIGHT AND BELOW St Paul's Cathedral, London (Sir Christopher Wren (1675–1710). This great cathedral was designed by a scientist with architectural genius. The high dome, surmounted by a masonry steeple, lantern and huge golden orb and cross, virtually seemed a structural impossibility in the late seventeenth century. Wren achieved his artistic ideal by using a clear and logical structure as the basis: the actual load-bearing dome is a conical brick structure (with oval holes to lessen its own weight) which transmits the weight of the lantern and outer dome downwards through flying buttresses round the base of the dome. The buttresses are hidden behind a Corinthian colonnade. The brick dome is also hidden; the awesome beauty of the dome's exterior and interior is created by deceptive shells. The outer dome is in fact a hemispherical veneer on timber framing, and the inner dome is saucer-shaped and much lower, supporting only itself.

ABOVE The Great Fire of London (1666) gave Wren the opportunity of redesigning the City: St Paul's was to provide the focal point. Clearly inspired by Italian Baroque, it is nevertheless a restrained and essentially Protestant answer to St Peter's.

Inside, the spatial qualities of the Baroque are more obvious.

ABOVE Syon House, London (Adam 1761). Many view Adam's greatest achievement as his skill as a decorator. While this may be unfair to his achievements in architecture, there is no doubt that his interiors were both popular and influential. This hall at Syon shows his superb handling of neo-Classical orders and decorations.

LEFT Osterley Park, Middlesex, England (1761–80). Robert Adam (1728–92). Adam imposed the new neo-Classicism on to the bones of an earlier building whose origins are shown by the corner towers. The architect cleverly filled the open courtyard front with a portico based on reconstructions of the Portico of Octavia of ancient Rome. The interior is meticulously detailed throughout.

■ baroque plasterwork

Most rendering and plastering is done by building up several layers of rough plaster and finishing with a fine layer floated off to a hard smooth surface. Long straight rules are used to regulate the overall flatness of the surface. Basic plasterer's tools have been in existence for centuries. The Roman architect Vitruvius described the spreading of stucco-duro with an iron trowel or float, and the smoothness of Egyptian plaster could only have been achieved with such equipment. The 1703 edition of Joseph Moxon's *Mechanick Exercises* describes and illustrates tools for plastering which are not unfamiliar to us today.

To make mouldings, plasterers use either "running moulds" or casting moulds. Running moulds are used to form continuous profiles such as cornices and skirtings. A template is cut from zinc, in the reverse and exact shape of the required profile. This is then mounted on a wooden support known as a "horse", which is run back and forth over a mound of wet plaster. The consistency and accuracy of line is achieved by running the horse along a fixed ground or a rule. This type of moulding can be done either in situ or on a bench. Complicated sections are usually built up from different mouldings run in short lengths and assembled later. Very heavy or thick sections are run over a formwork to leave a hollow space behind.

Casting in moulds is a workshop activity. The Adam brothers, Robert (1728–92) and James, used to use moulds carved from box or pear wood. But usually gelatine, wax or plaster were used for internal work and wood, iron or plaster for external; today, PVC is also used. By the mid-eighteenth century fibrous plaster was introduced in France. This consisted of plaster of Paris reinforced by a coarse canvas known as "scrim", in conjunction with wooden laths, wire netting, tow, fibre, sawdust and slag wood.

Stucco work in the Baroque period is noted for its exuberant and intricate scrolls, faces and caryatid figures. The details of such ceilings as that at Astley Hall, Chorley, were built over a structure of armatures (brackets and stems made of wood, leather and lead strips).

By the eighteenth century, native craftsmen had emerged in most European countries. In England, family firms, such as Joseph Rose and William Collins, began to work in close liaison with architects, such as the Adam brothers. A number of new recipes involving oils and alternative powders, such as cockle-shell lime, were invented. In 1777, the Adam brothers acquired the patents for two of the most important recipes and cornered the market in providing stucco decoration. Designs in similar style were made available through the general dissemination of pattern books. The stuccoed motifs were taken from boxwood moulds that could be used over and over again. The high relief exuberance of the Renaissance had been replaced by a technique that produced shallow relief of great delicacy; a suggestive veneer rather than the full-bodied imitation of stone architecture or sculpture, and with little more spirit than wallpaper.

ABOVE Heveningham Hall, Suffolk, England (1778). James Wyatt (1747–1813). Palladian elements contribute to the lightness of this orangery in a Classical house. It has a deceptively nineteenth-century appearance, a century which saw the great popularity of that descendant of the orangery – the conservatory.

► adam

Robert Adam was the second born of four brothers, all of whom were to become celebrated in the world of design and architecture. Their father was himself a leading Scottish architect, favouring a generally Palladian style. Following education in Edinburgh, Robert studied under his father before travelling to Rome for two years (1755–57), then touring the major architectural sites of Europe.

Soon after returning to England, he rapidly attained a tremendous reputation for interior and exterior design – so much so that in 1761 he was appointed architect of the king's works at the age of 33. His younger brother James joined him within two years, and together they published books of design that increased the already huge popularity of the Adams' style in building, decoration and furniture (including silverware and metalwork). Their interpretation of neo-Classicism was elegant and sophisticated, and was by far the most appreciated pattern of the day. Its influence spread quickly over much of Europe and to North America.

In terms of architecture, however, Robert was given few commissions to build new houses – most often he was asked to refurbish old ones or to redecorate the interiors. But there were exceptions, major ones being Harewood House, Nostell Priory and Home House (in London).

He died in March 1792 aged 63.

■ gothic revival

After the Renaissance broke up in Baroque extravaganza, architecture looked back to history for guidance. There followed a complete absence of originality, while architecture devoted itself to a reiteration of historical styles. From Greek and Gothic stone building stemmed two quite distinct types of architectural expression. It became a matter of taste as to which style was selected for a particular design. Having made the choice, architects used either style, or in some cases both styles, to design buildings expressing their own individuality.

John Nash (1752–1835), James Watt (1746–1813) and A. W. N. Pugin (1812–52) were the progenitors of the neo-Gothic style. For external use, Georgian architects such as Nash and Thomas Cubitt applied patent stuccoes over brickwork to provide impressive façades imitating expensive masonry. The addition of statuary and architectural stone carvings, made from the secret recipe of Coade Stone, took the general effect of make-believe a stage further.

The most famous of the patent external renderings was Parker's Roman Cement. It was said to have made Nash's architecture possible, due to its strength, durability and power to withstand damp. Carefully incised lines imitated stone coursing, and stone weathering was simulated with paint. From the 1820s, however, Portland cement gradually took over from the patent lime-based stucco mixtures.

BELOW Glyptothek, Munich, Germany (1816–34). von Klenze. A Greek revival sculpture gallery. This was the earliest of von Klenze's important commissions. The flat pediment heavily enriched with sculpture like the Parthenon, is typical of the period and bears comparison with the British Museum.

► nash

John Nash was born in London in 1752, the son of an engineer. At about the age of 16 he joined the office of the architect Sir Robert Taylor. Ten years later he set up in business for himself but within six years went bankrupt and moved to South Wales to make a fresh start. There he designed a number of country houses — and several jails — and gradually attained a modest reputation, on the strength of which he returned to London in 1796.

His marriage, two years later, seems to have opened a new chapter in Nash's life. It was at that time he obtained the patronage of the Prince Regent, and found himself with enough capital to remodel and live in a town house while also building himself the grand East Cowes Castle on the Isle of Wight.

Royal patronage brought him the commission of designing the residential area of London that became Regent Street and Regent's Park, and also included the Regent's canal, shops, houses, churches and arcades, and the street-plan for the entire district. Work began in 1811. Particularly noteworthy is the church of All Souls, Langham Place, and its circular portico of columns, and the grand terraces of Park Crescent and Carlton House Terrace.

In 1815 Nash was asked to extend and alter the Royal Pavilion in Brighton in outlandish "Hindoo" style; the interior was completely refurbished — and the cost was astronomical. In 1821 another royal property, Buckingham House, was scheduled for upgrading to become Buckingham Palace. The former Prince Regent, now George IV, declared that no expense should be spared on the interior and exterior reconstruction of the building. The king died before the work was completed, and Nash (who by that time shared the king's general unpopularity) was summarily dismissed.

Nash died at Cowes in May 1835.

ABOVE Carlton Terrace, London (John Nash). The picturesque style in architecture coincided with a renewed appreciation of the natural landscape in the arts generally.

ABOVE This "plantation Palladian" house in the southern states of America shows a typical use of timber to emulate stone construction. Inspired by the mansions of Renaissance Italy, themselves a revival of earlier classical traditions, such colonial mansions were built in the material that was to hand, and upon which the economy was based at that time.

■ the development of timber building in north america

In the seventeenth century, the last vestiges of the pure carpentry tradition were carried to America by the English colonists, where its regeneration was stimulated by contact with the skills of the many other immigrant nationalities. House plans originating in eastern England dominated, but a rapid transition took place from half-timber framing to lightweight framed panels, particularly on the eastern seaboard. Comparison with European examples is made easier by the sheer size of the country and the resulting isolation of various ethnic and cultural groups – the Puritan sects in Pennsylvania preserve to this day the structural forms and community involvement in building which originated in Europe.

In the northern half of the United States, both the size and the plan of most early houses are fairly uniform, and original East Anglian framing methods persisted. However, the wattle-and-daub infilling panels were soon replaced by the more appropriate clapboard – a system of horizontal timber cladding over the wooden framework that emphasized the building style's clean, crisp lines, especially when further accentuated by external shutters on the windows. The widespread influence of the classical Renaissance is apparent in the shaping and painting of woodwork to imitate stone on many eighteenth-century houses.

Gradually, this influence lessened. Towards the latter part of the nineteenth century, innovators like Henry H. Richardson (1838–86) created their own architectural vocabulary and used it to produce the "shingle style" – a free internal design approach using the flexibility of the wooden shingle as its outward expression, as seen in the resort towns of the New England coast.

Further south, social differences were more marked, the social order ranging from company or plantation bosses to slaves. The variety of timber buildings reflects this. The large "plantation Palladian" mansions are a truly indigenous form but most smaller buildings are very similar to English or Dutch prototypes. Gradually the warmer climate influenced a different approach to general design. This led to the introduction of more open plans employing screens and verandahs to link inside and outside spaces.

Today, the majority of Americans still live in timber houses and wood is still the cheapest building material.

RIGHT Clifton Suspension Bridge, Bristol, England (Brunel, 1830–59). A magnificent early bridge across the Avon Gorge. The massive Egyptian-like pylons were unusual at the time, owing little to contemporary architecture.

BELOW Métro Station, Paris (Hector Guimard). Designed at the turn of the century, these underground station entrances contain all the long, tenuous curves in iron so favoured by the architects of the Art Nouveau.

■ iron – the new material

Renaissance buildings made use of iron for tie rods across arches and for chains around domes, but it was the introduction of coke-smelted iron in England in 1747 that raised the quality and lowered the price of cast-iron so that it could be used for major building elements. Between 1770 and 1772, St. Anne's Church in Liverpool was built with cast-iron columns, and during the next half-century the

material was developed first for bridges over the Severn and then for nearby factories in Shrewsbury and Derbyshire.

The first major cast-iron structure to be built was the 100-foot (30 m) span Iron Bridge at Coalbrookdale, now within the boundary of the new town of Telford. It was in October 1775 that Thomas Pritchard, a Shrewsbury architect, first suggested that the proposed bridge at Coalbrookdale be constructed of cast-iron. He was in the right part of the world for this idea to be taken up, for Abraham Darby had pioneered the use of coke for smelting at Coalbrookdale and his son was probably the only man in the world who could build the bridge, with its main ribs reaching halfway across the river and each weighing 5¾ tons. There were no precedents for the construction of this bridge. Abraham Darby and his son-in-law, Richard Reynolds, had to work everything out for themselves – bolts, rivets and welding were all in the future. They evolved techniques of joining where members were slotted one into the other and secured by iron wedges.

It is not easy to work something out from scratch, and just as the early railway engineers designed trains like a string of stage coaches, so Darby and Reynolds borrowed the arch form of a masonry bridge. Nevertheless, the bridge is beautifully constructed and stands today as an elegant reminder of the skill of the early ironmasters, and of their bravery in designing and building such a structure before it was generally known how to calculate structural materials.

The Coalbrookdale bridge might have remained an isolated example of iron bridgebuilding, but, in 1787, the 30-year-old engineer Thomas Telford (1757–1834) was appointed Surveyor of Public Works for Shropshire. The Coalbrookdale bridge fell into this parish and Telford soon abandoned his mason's training and enthusiastically took up cast-iron. His bridge at nearby Buildwas spanned 123 feet (40 m), yet weighed only half as much as the Coalbrookdale bridge.

The construction of the early cast-iron bridges coincided with the building of the first factories. The type of building constructed to house the new industries had already been set by John Lombe's silk mill built in Derby in 1718. In 1769, Richard Arkwright (1732–1792) patented his water frame, which set the British textile industry on a century of world supremacy and produced a situation where small-scale operations were no longer economic; from the time of this patent, work was increasingly concentrated and the factory, a new building type, came onto the scene. The early factories were built by Arkwright and his licencees, and they were spaced along rivers, such as the Derwent, wherever a change in water level generated enough power to turn the water wheels.

The Arkwright mills of the last 30 years of the eighteenth century followed the model of John Lombe's Derby mill, with four, five or six storeys, brick or stone outside walls and heavy timber frames. With a young and often tired workforce, oil lighting and an inflammable product in a timber-framed building, fire was more than a hazard, it was

RIGHT Karlsplatz station, Vienna Stadtbahn (Otto Wagner, 1894–7). Wagner was commissioned to devise a scheme for the replanning of the centre of Vienna; the Stadtbahn was the sole element to come to fruition.

a certainty. One after another of Arkwright's mills were destroyed by fire within a year or two of completion. The entire development of the Industrial Revolution in England was held up by the lack of fireproof mills.

William Strutt (1756–1830), a millowner and son of Arkwright's partner, was the first to tackle the problem. His calico mill of 1793 in Derby was six storeys high and measured 115 × 33 feet (35 × 10 m). Columns were cast-iron, of cruciform section to give maximum strength without the casting difficulties of hollow, round columns. Timber beams spanned between these columns and between these were vaults of hollow pot construction levelled with sand and paved with bricks. The underside of the timber beam, which would otherwise have been exposed, was plastered and then covered with sheet metal for fire protection.

In 1786, Victor Louis roofed the Théâtre Français in Paris with an iron frame. In spite of revolution and war, news of this encouraged Strutt to proceed with the development of the iron-framed mill. Although Strutt had advanced most of the way to the fireproof mill, metal-covered timber was something of a makeshift. It remained for Charles Bage, who knew William Strutt and Telford, to take one of the major steps forward in building technology, by making a building with the internal construction completely framed in metal. This flax mill, at Shrewsbury, was finished in 1797 and still exists.

William Strutt quickly followed Bage with his own North Mill at Belper completed in 1803. This is probably the fourth metal-framed building ever built, and it was splendidly serviced. It was ventilated by passing air, heated in winter, through ducts discharging through adjustable registers. Belper North Mill is six storeys high, the top floor reserved for a Sunday school for the young workforce.

The Bage mill had a Boulton and Watt steam engine and these engineers, Matthew Boulton and James Watt, were not slow to realize the developments that were taking place. When they were commissioned to construct a new mill in Manchester for the Salford Twist Company, they developed the cast-iron frame for a much larger building than Bage's and to a much greater degree of sophistication. It was heated by steam passing through hollow columns and beams, and lit by gas. The completion of a building of such quality in Manchester set the standard, and cast-iron construction became normal.

All of these mills had outer walls of brick or stone. There are various claimants to being the first to construct the completely metal-frame multistorey building. In 1840, the greatest of the English mill builders, William Fairbairn, built a prefabricated mill with outside walls of iron plates and shipped it to Istanbul for erection there; and in 1849 the American James Bogardus (1800–1874) built a factory at Center and Duane Streets in New York entirely in glass and iron, Italian Renaissance in style.

Fairbairn's Istanbul mill and Bogardus' factory both disappeared long ago and few records remain, but it is probable that both buildings used masonry to take wind and other non-vertical loads. The oldest all-metal frame multi-storey building, with rigid connections to take wind loads, is probably the four-storey Sheerness Boathouse of 1858–60, a magnificent building, which is unfortunately difficult to visit as it is in the Naval Dockyard. The designer of the boathouse, Colonel Godfrey Greene, had previously employed the contractors who built the Crystal Palace and had been influenced by their expertise. The Boatstore is clad in corrugated iron, and it was the first building to use the I-sections which are standard in structural steelwork today. A dozen years later, the Menier Chocolate Company built a factory, the Turbine Building, astride three turbines in the river at Noisiel-sur-Marne in France. Here the frame uses diagonal members to ensure rigidity without elaborate connections.

► eiffel

Alexandre Gustave Eiffel is most famous for the eyecatching tower he constructed in Paris for the *Exposition Universelle* of 1889. But the tower is, in fact, a masterpiece that came relatively late in his long life. It has been described as a monument to 19th-century engineering skill, although Eiffel lived on, still working, well into the 20th century.

Eiffel was born in Dijon in December 1832. He attended the college of art and engineering in Paris, and there became totally fascinated by the physics and engineering involved in the building of bridges. The manufacture of structures that could span distances horizontally and vertically became his single specialty. He was also concerned to ensure that the bridges he built had an aesthetic quality of airiness about them – which, because it entailed fewer constructive elements, also added to the economy inherent in his designs. Major works include the bridge over the River Douro in Portugal, and the Garabit viaduct in southern France.

Because he was experienced in constructing strong framework while retaining an element of lightness, Eiffel was commissioned in 1855 to design the inner structure that would act as the framework for the Statue of Liberty, presented by France to the United States.

The Eiffel tower of Paris was begun shortly afterwards, and combined all the expertise gained throughout Eiffel's career to date.

Thereafter he mostly confined himself to experiments in the construction of light frames for aircraft, and in the physics of flight – a science that was in its infancy at that time. His first wind tunnel, built for his own aerodynamics laboratory, was erected in 1912 – when he was aged 80.

He died in Paris in December 1923.

In 1790, Robert Owen had successfully spun American cotton by machine. At once it became obvious to Americans that they could emulate this British success, and spin their own cotton in their own country. In 1793, Sam Slater, who had been employed in Arkwright and Strutt's Belper mill, built America's first cotton mill at Pawtucket, Rhode Island, powered by water from the Blackstone River. Slater had left Belper before the arrival of the fireproof mills, and the Pawtucket building was built out of heavy timbers. The early American mills had outside walls of timber with shiplap boarding and the fire hazard in New England proved to be just as great.

When iron construction did come to American mill builders, fresh problems were in store for them, for the young republic did not have the skills, either at calculating or casting iron, that existed in England at that time. Columns were cast on their sides, and this meant that the core mould could slip out of alignment, so that a column taking a heavy load might have paper-thin iron on one side. Such columns, cast by the Eagle Iron Foundry, were used in the interior construction of Pemberton Mill, Lawrence, Massachusetts. The structure was perfectly fireproof, but, in 1860, it collapsed under its own weight, killing 200 people. This disaster discouraged builders from using iron; American mill engineers preferred timber construction until the end of the nineteenth century.

ABOVE The bold skeletal structure of the Eiffel Tower (Gustave Eiffel, 1889) – a clear precursor of the High Tech movement.

■ steel

Cast-iron as a bulding material arrived in the laissez-faire world of eighteenth and early nineteenth-century Britain, but by the time steel arrived a century later, governmental control affected the use of the material. While the use of cast-iron had spread rapidly and indiscriminately, and was used with great flair leading to some dramatic disasters, the spread of steel was a slow and carefully monitored process, mercifully free from disasters, but often inhibited by bureaucratic obstinacy. In 1859, the engineer John Hawkshaw (1811–1891) proposed to use structural steel for his Charing Cross railway bridge in London, but he was refused permission by the Board of Trade who, for the next 20 years, would not allow steel to be used for shipbuilding or for structural work. It was left to the Dutch and the Americans to pioneer the use and further development of the new Bessemer steel.

The first bridge using Bessemer steel was built in Holland in 1865, and the qualities of the material were fully demonstrated by Captain James B. Eads (1820–1887) in his beautiful bridge over the Mississippi at St. Louis, opened in 1874. The Eads bridge used Carnegie-Kloman chrome steel and launched Andrew Carnegie's career as a steelmaker. Some of the structural members of the Eads bridge were iron, but four years later, General William Sooy Smith spanned the Missouri at Glasgow, South Dakota, with a bridge entirely constructed of steel members.

In Britain, the Admiralty were not affected by the Board of Trade restrictions and, after 1870, all major warships were built of steel. In 1877, the Board of Trade realized that steel could not be banned forever and appointed a committee (of only three men) to advise on the use of structural steel; the committee reported favourably on the merits of the new material. Arguments continued, but the use of steel was finally permitted in time for its use on a grand scale in the Forth Bridge (1883–90), designed by John Fowler and Benjamin Baker.

The expense of setting up a rolling mill was so great that steel was marketed in standard sections, unlike cast iron where special moulds for individually designed pieces presented no problem. The use of standard rolled sections, combined with the very high degree of reliability of the material, led to codified design procedures, and tables in which engineers could look up the load-bearing capacities of different steel members. The Phoenix Iron Company produced the first such handbook in the United States in 1869. This was followed by the Carnegie *Pocket Companion* in 1873, which became the manual for steel designers around the world.

In 1883, construction was started on the Statue of Liberty, which had a copper skin over a steel frame designed by Gustave Eiffel (1832–1923) and reaching up 147 feet (45 m). However, the first major use of steel in a conventional structure was probably William Le Baron Jenney's Home Insurance Building in Chicago, completed in 1885 and demolished in 1931.

In Jenney's Home Insurance Building, often claimed as the first true metal-framed high-rise building, the first five floors were built with cast-iron columns and wrought-iron beams, but the next five floors were built with Carnegie steel beams. Two additional steel floors were added in 1889.

Jenney followed his success with the Second Leiter Building (later the Sears Roebuck store) at State and Van Buren Streets. This building has a much more relaxed appearance than the Home Insurance and lacks the heavy base. Jenney's Fair Store at Adams and State Streets (1891) used steel for columns as well as beams. His Manhattan Building of the same year at 431 South Dearborn Street had a lighter structure, so that wind loads became a more significant factor – these are accepted through the frame by deep connections on the upper floors and by concealed steel diagonals at ground level. It was another 50 years before architects became brave enough to expose the diagonals needed to brace the tall frame.

Jenney was the structural innovator, but it was the young men trained in his office who gave clear architectural expression to the technical expertise he taught them. The Tacoma Building of 1889 by Holabird & Roche introduced rivetted connections. They followed this with the Marquette Building, still standing at 140 South Dearborn Street. Daniel Burnham's office produced the beautiful Reliance Building (1894), a faceted glass tower at 32 North State Street. But the most skilled of all were Dankmar Adler (1844–1900), and Louis Sullivan, whose Wainwright Building at St. Louis (1891), Guaranty building at Buffalo, New York (1895) and Carson Pirie & Scott store in Chicago (1898), brought the fire-proofed metal frame to as clear an expression as was possible with the means of the time.

The first complete steel-frame high-rise building in New York was probably the American Surety Building at Broadway and Pine Street designed by Bruce Price. Its 20 storeys took it to a height of 295 feet (90 m).

Following the success of the Tacoma and the American Surety, there was nothing to stop skyscrapers from growing and growing – and that is precisely what they did.

RIGHT Second Leiter Building (1889–91, William Le Baron Jenney). Jenney was one of the foremost pioneers of high-rise construction in buildings with steel frames.

LEFT Paddington Station, London (Brunel, 1852). Brunel was the pioneer designer of bridges, ships and railway stations. The Industrial Revolution is elegantly displayed in this curved span of steel trusses supported on cast-iron columns.

▶ pugin

Augustus Welby Northmore Pugin was born in March 1812, the son of a fairly well-known architectural illustrator, by whom he was educated and trained. At the age of 20 his father died, and Pugin spent the following four years travelling through England, France and the Low Countries, studying medieval art and architecture and publishing (with R. Ackermann) four volumes of designs of Gothic furniture, metalwork and household ornaments.

He became a Roman Catholic during these years, which played an important role in the development of his work. From 1837 many of the commissions Pugin was offered were from Roman Catholic laymen and clergy, notably John Talbot, Earl of Shrewsbury. Churches he designed at this time include St Chad's Cathedral, Birmingham and St George's Cathedral, Southwark. His church of St Oswald, Old Swan, Liverpool, actually established the pattern for Gothic revival churches in the country (although it was later demolished).

From 1840 to 1844, Pugin was at the height of his considerable powers as an architect and also as a well-known author, designer, theorist and antiquarian. Many elegant and innovative variants on the old Gothic style were devised at this time.

But his second wife died in 1844, and Pugin – although he remarried – was never the same again. His mental health deteriorated and despite his remaining professionally active, his practice declined markedly. Finally he became seriously mentally ill, and died suddenly in September 1852 at the age of 40.

RIGHT Law Courts, London (1868–82) G.E. Street (1824–81). A one-time assistant in Scott's office, Street continued a personal and somewhat severe Gothic Revival style. The Law Courts, won in competition in 1866, show how he combined his austere detailing with great freedom of facade treatment. The result is never dull and always impressive.

▶ george gilbert scott

Sir George Gilbert Scott (who has to be so called in order to distinguish him from his equally famous architect grandson Sir Giles Gilbert Scott) is probably best known for having designed the Albert Memorial in London in 1862. But by then he was more than 50 years old and had been eminent in his profession for more than two decades.

Scott was born in July 1811 in Buckinghamshire. After an apprenticeship with a London architect, his first of a great number of commissions to design a church came in 1838. However, his ideas changed once he had read the architectural theories of Augustus Pugin, who strongly advocated a return to Gothic values. Pugin's neo-Gothic influence is clearly evident in Scott's Martyrs' Memorial at Oxford (1841).

But it was the neo-Gothic design with which Scott won a competition for the new Nikolaikirche in Hamburg in 1844 that provoked international attention, and he began a career of glittering successes that today seem rather exaggerated for the actual architectural input involved. For all the fame and fortune, however, Scott was extremely hard-working, and was a prolific producer of original designs based on one predominant premise. In particular he organized the restoration or refurbishment of several medieval cathedrals and abbeys that had been long neglected, notably Lichfield, Salisbury and Ely Cathedrals and Westminster Abbey. This was not always to the approval of succeeding generations, it must be said. He was also responsible for the design of the great St Pancras Station Hotel in London.

He received his knighthood in 1872, and died in March 1878, aged 66.

TOP Houses of Parliament, London (1840–60). Charles Barry (1795–1860) & Pugin. Barry, essentially a Classical architect, won the rebuilding in a competition. His young assistant, Pugin, a fervent Gothicist, became responsible for most of the interior work which is in the Perpendicular style. The building became influential in establishing the credentials of the Gothic Revival.

ABOVE RIGHT Leighton House, London (Lord Leighton & Aitchison, 1877–79). A Victorian version of Persian architecture. This was the painter Leighton's own house, built at a time when exotic Eastern styles were popular, particularly in interiors. The workmanship and attention to detail make this a rewarding experience.

ABOVE Albert Memorial, London (Scott, 1864). The architecture may be impeccable Gothic but the effect, enhanced by the mosaic decorations, is overwhelmingly High Victorian. Nevertheless much of the detail is worth study.

▶ morris

Primarily perhaps an art theorist and author, William Morris is best known in the architectural world for his inventive contribution to decoration and interior design, and for his pioneering stance on the preservation of ancient buildings.

Born in Essex in March 1824 into a comparatively wealthy family, Morris was educated at Marlborough and then at Oxford University. At Oxford he formed a lifelong friendship with Edward Burne-Jones, with whom he spent vacations in France and Belgium studying art and Gothic architecture. Having gained his degree, in 1856 Morris entered the workshop of the architect G. E. Street, where Philip Webb — also to become a lifelong friend and colleague — was the senior clerk. The same year, Burne-Jones and Morris met Dante Gabriel Rossetti, and under his influence Morris determined to become a painter. With Rossetti he left London to assist in the decoration of the Oxford Union Society's new debating hall.

In 1859 Morris married Jane Burden (who became a frequent model for Rossetti's paintings) and moved to Upton, Kent. There he built The Red House, designed by himself and Webb in an innovatively simple brick style, with furniture also to his own design. Morris had found his true vocation.

In 1861 he founded the manufacturing company of Morris, Marshall, Faulkner & Co., and took premises in Red Lion Square, Bloomsbury. With Rossetti, Burne-Jones, Ford Madox Brown and others, Morris began to hand-produce the furniture, stained glass, wallpapers, tapestries and other decorative fabrics that were soon to influence Victorian tastes and standards. This was, of course, totally against the machine ethic of the age, which advocated cheap mass-production. Mass-production — and specifically production for the masses — was also Morris's goal, but production of these hand-crafted items could not be cheap, and to that extent this initial realization of the ideals of the Arts and Crafts Movement can be said to have failed.

However, it was the superb craftsmanship, the harmony and simplicity of the styling and decoration, and the long-lasting quality of the materials, that captivated Victorian sensibilities. The company flourished — it was to stay in business until 1940 — and was highly influential in the development of the decorative arts for decades thereafter.

Morris moved back to London and then in 1871 bought a country house at Lechlade, Oxfordshire (at first sharing the house also with Rossetti). It was there he was buried, after dying in London in October 1896 just three months after the publication of the last and finest of his illustrated books: *Chaucer*.

ABOVE The Red House, Bexleyheath, Kent (Philip Webb, 1859). The interior is more forward-looking than the outside, incorporating features which later became the currency of the Arts and Crafts Movement. The striking, fitted cupboards with their decorative hinges are by Morris.

FAR RIGHT One of the important early buildings of the English Domestic Revival, The Red House brought back simplicity in the form of a cosy grouping around a well.

TOP John Vassal House, Cambridge, USA (1759). A fine New England house. English and Dutch styles predominate, but the clapboard and shutters show the emergence of a national style.

ABOVE Wood House, Long Island, USA (19th cent). The direct Georgian simplicity of domestic houses had, by mid-century, ecome more elaborate, even ostentatious. Growing national prosperity saw the building of country houses outside New York for the wealthy business families to spend the summer.

■ contemporary american architecture

Out in the American countryside, architectural development followed the railways westward and led to the establishment of townships where no community had previously existed. Timber was the obvious choice for building in most cases and the elements of the familiar "wild west" main street became so stereotyped that standard plans were available.

By 1900, all constituent materials of American houses looked alike, whether the houses were made of brick, stone or wood. The vast amount of timber which was used was in the form of joinery, both externally and internally. By this time, too, communications had made the scenery and semi-tropical climate of southern California accessible to all with the wealth or ambition to travel. In this ideal environment, the brothers C.S. and H.M. Greene (1868–1957 and 1870–1954) developed their Californian bungalow style using the Bengalese houses of India as a starting point. Blending architectural skill, a sound knowledge of the fine arts and superb craftsmanship they produced results such as the Gamble house (1909) in Pasadena.

Comparisons are inevitably made between the Greenes' work and the work of Frank Lloyd Wright (1869–1959) but the Greenes were part of the Arts and Crafts Movement, while Wright was exploring ideas which would lead to the development of the "Prairie School" of organic architecture. Until then, in North America, if not the whole of Europe, architecture was based on Greek influence. "Organic" architecture had much more in common with the Oriental, mainly Buddhist, influences of early civilizations in India, Persia, China and Japan.

In the East, material was vital to the style of building but the style had evolved entirely from ceremonial organization of space and its relationship with nature. Frank Lloyd Wright said, "Americans, in seeking culture, could not accept that posts and beams could be thrown away in favour of folding or movable planes, nor that organic architecture could derive from the tall grass of the mid-western prairie. So the idea went round the world to find recognition and was then 'imported' to its own home as a thing to be imitated everywhere." Imitation was often shallow and inappropriate and generally involved wood, so it is no wonder there is some confusion regarding the role of timber construction in this period.

In terms of more conventional architecture relating to city buildings, American architects during the middle years of the nineteenth century introduced a Greek-style revival. Works of this kind included Thomas Cole's Ohio State Capital at Columbus, William Strickland's Tennessee State Capital at Nashville, Pollard's Courthouse at Petersburg, Va., and Thomas Walter's Girard College, Philadelphia. At the same time other styles were explored – such as the Egyptian in John Haviland's New York City Halls of Justice; the medieval by Alexander Jackson Davis in a number of houses and villas, and by Richard Upjohn in his Trinity church, lower Manhattan; and the Italian Palazzo by Upjohn again in his Edward King house on Long Island.

In the 1860s important public buildings were more likely to adopt the French Second-Empire architectural style.

Alfred Mullet was the most prolific of designers in this genre, while Frank Furness was an important designer of a more exotic variety of taste.

From about that time too, Henry Hobson Richardson – popularly known as the "father of American architecture" – employed a style based largely on Romanesque elements which were thought to echo the rugged individuality and constructive energy of the American people. This influenced his successors – notably Louis Sullivan and, through him, Frank Lloyd Wright – although Richardson was himself to turn his interests in another direction.

Partnerships were of great importance just before the turn of the twentieth century in the United States. Some of the greatest architectural commissions of all were entrusted to partnerships such as Bunham & Root and the important firm of McKim, Mead & White.

▶ richardson

Henry Hobson Richardson is credited with being the initiator of the Romanesque revival in North America and also with being a pioneer in the development of an architectural style that was both modern and truly American. In Romanesque and in modern styles – which are of course very different from each other – he was singularly successful.

Richardson was born in St. James, La., in September, 1838. His education was completed at Harvard and was succeeded by study at the Ecole des Beaux Arts in Paris, France. He returned to the United States in 1865, but retained a feel for the French Romanesque style he had seen in Paris, and it was in that style that he designed the Trinity church in Boston (1872) which made his name.

By 1887, when he designed the Marshall Field Wholesale Building in Chicago, his style had become audacious and personal: rows of tall, arched windows emphasized stern and generally undecorated lines; the choice of materials was distinctive and skilful. This style is evident also in the Ames-Pray Building in Boston, and is said to herald the style devised later by Louis Sullivan.

Other notable buildings for which Richardson was responsible include the Pittsburgh Courthouse and Jail, Sever Hall at Harvard University, and Stoughton House, Cambridge, Mass.

Richardson died in Boston, aged only 47, in April 1886.

LEFT Trinity Church, Boston, USA (1873–77). Henry Richardson (1838–86). Richardson was born in Louisiana and went to study in Paris, a background reflected in his architecture in which French and English forms of Romanesque and Gothic combine. Trinity Church, won in competition, is a massive but personal essay in Romanesque, brutally detailed in pink granite and rough ashlar.

■ the chicago school

The great American contribution to building in iron was not made in mill construction but in office buildings, and not on the East Coast, but in Chicago in the 1870s and 1880s. Mid-nineteenth century Chicago was a boom town. Buildings were constructed of timber, with some cast-iron columns and beams, and with little serious study of the problem of fire. In 1871, the centre of the city was burnt to the ground in 48 hours, and in the heat of the fire, iron structural members melted, the running molten iron contributing to the spread of the fire. The city centre was destroyed and 100,000 people made homeless.

In the ruins of the city stood the nearly completed Nixon Building, designed by Otto Matz, at La Salle and Monroe Streets; the builders cleaned it down and completed it in two months. The triumphant success of the Nixon Building was due to its masonry external walls, and to the fact that the iron members of its internal frame were fireproofed with a layer of concrete or plaster. The next year, hollow

ABOVE Carson Pirie & Scott department store, Chicago (Louis Sullivan, 1899–1904). For Sullivan, even the relatively subtle expression of the building's cellular structure was a bold gesture.

terracotta blocks were introduced for floor construction, for building partitions and for encasing the structural iron. Efficient, economical fireproofing had arrived and was first used for the Kendall Building at 40 North Dearborn Street, completed in 1873.

Among those engaged in the frenetic rebuilding of Chicago's commercial district was the engineer William Le Baron Jenney (1832–1907). His First Leiter Building of 1879, still standing at Wells and Monroe Street, takes some of the loads on the outside walls on iron members – almost true skeleton construction. It also shows mastery of the architectural expression of this type of construction – all windows and piers on all floors look alike, indicating the repetitive nature of a framed building, as opposed to traditional load-bearing structures, where walls became thicker nearer the ground.

In 1885, Jenney built the Home Insurance Building at La Salle and Adams Streets, a building best-known for its use of steel. The architectural expression of the iron frame is not nearly so clear as the First Leiter Building, but the structure was "pure" skeleton – all loads were taken on the metal frame. The building was no beauty, but Jenney made two great contributions: he instigated safe metal framing, whereby subsequent skyscrapers were and still are constructed, and he trained in his office the men who would design the beautiful Chicago skyscrapers of the next generation – Louis Sullivan (1856–1924), William Holabird (1854–1923), Martin Roche (1855–1927) and Daniel Burnham (1846–1912).

LEFT Fisher Building, Chicago (Daniel Burnham, 1895). More decorative than most buildings of the Chicago School the Fisher Building shows elements of that style – a clearly expressed regular frame, and bay windows to catch the light in narrow city streets. By 1895 the metal framing technique had been mastered in Chicago: once out of the ground the framing to the Fisher Building went up at the rate of a floor a day.

▶ louis sullivan

Louis Henry Sullivan has been described as one of the pioneers of the Modern movement in American architecture. His greatest work was undoubtedly done during his fifteen-year partnership with Dankmar Adler (1881–1895).

Sullivan was born in Boston, Mass., and was educated at MIT, at Cambridge in England and at the Ecole des Beaux Arts in Paris, France. At one stage thereafter, back in the United States, he worked in the draught-office of William Le Baron Jenney who soon afterwards devised the principles which made the construction of skyscrapers possible.

It was just at the time of that discovery that Sullivan joined Adler, and within the fifteen years they were in partnership, the two designed more than a hundred buildings together. Particularly noteworthy are the Auditorium Building, the Gage Building and the Transportation Building for the Columbian Exposition, all in Chicago. Another two great skyscrapers for which the partnership was responsible were the Wainwright Building in St. Louis, Mo., and the Prudential Building in Buffalo, N.Y.

Towards the end of the partnership, Sullivan took on a young apprentice: he was Frank Lloyd Wright, who was to become even more celebrated as an architect, yet who always referred to Sullivan as "the Master". Wright was strongly influenced by Sullivan's ideas on harmony of design and the careful choice of appropriate materials both in structural elements and in decoration, particularly in steel-framed buildings. Later Sullivan was to popularize these ideas in several books on the philosophy of architectural design.

When his partnership with Adler came to an end, much of Sullivan's practice did too. Nevertheless he was responsible for designing the Carson Pirie Scott department store in Chicago (1899) and several stylish banks in small midwestern towns. But he died in abject poverty in Chicago in April 1924. He was posthumously awarded the gold medal of the American Institute of Architects in 1943

ABOVE Reliance Building, Chicago, USA (Burnham & Root, 1890–95). A glimpse of the future, anticipating the curtain wall with its large proportion of glass to solid. The modelling of the facade is particularly successful. Chicago is a windy city and the internal bracing took account of this.

ABOVE Gage Building, Chicago, USA (Holabird & Roche, 1898). Facade by Sullivan. The familiar sinuous decorations are treated almost like capitals on the central pilasters.

LEFT Auditorium Building, Chicago, USA (Adler & Sullivan, 1886–90). Sullivan returned to Chicago from a brief period of study in Paris and set up a partnership with Dankmar Adler. This, their first major building, brought them instant success. Its load-bearing stone facade owes much to Richardson, carefully tiered in a Renaissance manner to break up its huge mass. The interior decoration is also by Sullivan.

■ the age of the skyscraper

How will the twentieth century be judged by the future historians of architecture? To some extent, that question is inextricably tied to the destiny of human civilization.

For example, is it possible to imagine that a future century could spawn such a dramatic pace of technological change as has produced first the wireless telegraph and then the super-computer? If not, then how could architecture again stride the distance between the Carson, Pirie & Scott department store and the Hongkong & Shanghai Bank in the space of 100 years?

Indeed, set against an age that has seen the splitting of the atom and men landing on the moon, the speed at which architecture has changed this century may seem less impressive.

However, it will be difficult for future chroniclers of architectural history to conclude that the twentieth century has been anything less than revolutionary. It is a time when architecture has become truly international for the first time, when local influences have been subordinated to a global style, and when the traditions of East and West have converged.

The buildings of today are constructed using many materials that had not been invented 100 years ago, and the role of the craftsman in their creation has been largely superseded by factory mass-production. And the architects of this century have found new masters. No longer the exlusive servants of governments and wealthy patrons, architects have found themselves as often designing factories and office headquarters for international corporations, or housing and amenities for the masses.

Like many of the arts, architecture in the twentieth century has sometimes appeared perilously close to self-destruction, and certainly in the last few decades has fragmented into increasingly numerous 'isms'.

The story of twentieth century architecture is primarily, however, the story of the modern movement, Modernism spent the early part of the century finding its feet, the middle asserting itself, and in latter years has been fighting a rearguard action in order to survive against the swing of popular opinion.

After trying so hard to shake off the legacy of a tradition that stretches back to classical times, architecture now finds itself steering an uneven path, pulled in one direction by the children of Modernism, and in the opposite direction by those who would see a return to historical roots. Perhaps

TOP Housing, Silver End, Essex, England (1927). Thomas Tait (1882–1954). It was almost de rigeur to build modern houses in concrete or rendered brickwork. The new steel windows were also an essential part.

ABOVE 64 Old Church Street, Chelsea, London (Mendelsohn & Chermayeff, 1936). A restrained town house. The exaggerated horizontality of the ground floor forms a long podium for the simpler treatment of the upper storey.

the true judge of the twentieth century will be time itself, and its verdict will be delivered in the extent to which Modernism survives into the next millennium.

At the turn of the twentieth century, the roots of modern architecture had already been planted in the steel-framed, multistorey commercial buildings by Louis Sullivan, Henry H. Richardson and others, mainly in Chicago, St. Louis and Buffalo, in the 1880s and 1890s. But it was to take another 20-odd years, and a war that was to change the world, before the spirit of 'Modernism' began to find a coherent style that it could call its own.

The years between were a time of experimentation, of ideas that veered between unprecedented social responsibility and escapist fantasy, and often of retreat into traditional ways. But the ground covered in the pre-World War I years was as great as that covered in entire centuries before.

During the nineteenth century, a number of factors conspired to create the pressure for a modern style of architecture. Continuing industrialization led to a need for new kinds of buildings, while the rapid growth in urban populations obliged architects to build upwards. Political reforms and the growing popularity of socialist ideals led people to question established values in every aspect of life, and to look for new artistic forms that expressed the changes in human society. By the end of the century, the

materials and technology necessary to create a new architecture were also available.

The use of prefabricated cast-iron and wrought-iron components had been mastered by the middle of the century, in such buildings as Joseph Paxton's 1851 Crystal Palace in London. By the 1880s, Bessemer's new smelting techniques had enabled steel frames to be easily manufactured. Electric elevators, essential to transport people quickly up and down the new skyscrapers, were in operation by the 1890s. Most important of all, though, was the development of reinforced concrete, largely the work of François Hennebique in France. Reinforced concrete enabled huge distances to be spanned, and allowed construction of many buildings that would otherwise have been impossible.

By the start of the twentieth century, the architectural establishment was ripe for change. For too long it had been dominated by historicism – the routine and often academic imitation of historical styles, with an emphasis on ornamentation. Britain's Arts and Crafts Movement, in its quest to rediscover the simplicity of vernacular architecture, had been the first attempt to break the hold of historicism.

Art Nouveau became the first reaction on an international scale. Although with hindsight it may be regarded as a false start, there is no doubting the liberating effect that it achieved.

LEFT Sun House, London (1936). Maxwell Fry (b1899). Skilful English practitioner of the Bauhaus style, as shown in this assured example in Hampstead. The house has reinforced concrete walls, steel columns to support the balconies and extensive glazing.

ABOVE Bounds Green Station, London (Adams, Holden & Pearson, 1933). Charles Holden was the key figure in the partnership which was responsible for more than 30 London Underground stations. Never a thorough-going Modernist – he had trained under the Arts and Crafts architect, Ashbee – Holden nevertheless developed what might be called neo-Classical Modernism in which greatly simplified Classical elements were employed.

ABOVE Woolworth Building, New York (1913). Cass Gilbert (1859–1934). Gilbert strove to impose traditional forms to the skyscraper. Gothic, with its emphasis on the vertical, seemed appropriate, and there is no doubt the Woolworth Tower is one of the best considered of all city skyscrapers. Long out of favour for its architectural "dishonesty", it now enjoys deserved appreciation.

RIGHT Municipal Building Center, New York (McKim, Mead & White, 1913). Although lively enough in its general modelling, this building exposes one of the great problems of the skyscraper — what to do with the middle storeys. The top and bottom are interesting enough, but in-between is distinctly arid.

BELOW Empire State Building, New York (Shreve, Lamb & Harmon, 1930). The skyscraper tower par excellence. For some time the tallest building in the world. Its commercial success, coinciding with the Depression, was for a time in jeopardy. In detail it is dull, but the buttressing of the upper storeys and Art Deco Gothic spire are well handled.

LEFT Wrigley Building, Chicago, USA (Graham, Anderson, Probst & White, 1921). The criticism of unrelieved central storeys applies to this commercial building, though the windows are well proportioned.

RIGHT Glasgow School of Art (Charles Rennie Mackintosh, 1896–1908). Mackintosh's most original building. The influence of Art Nouveau is in the detail, rather than the overall impression.

■ art nouveau

Art Nouveau was an international reaction against the backward-looking historicism that had passed for nineteenth-century architecture. Inspired by the imagery of organic structures like plant-forms and marine life, Art Nouveau was characterized by sinuous, curving lines that appeared in various undulating and interlaced patterns. It was a style that was readily adopted in many branches of design including textiles, glassware and jewellery. To its supporters it represented a daring challenge to the architectural establishment's sterile practice of endlessly reviving Renaissance and Classical styles. To its detractors, it seldom overcame the charge of being mere surface decoration, and was unworthy of the status of a truly architectural movement.

By common consensus, the first true example of Art Nouveau design was the title page by Arthur Mackmurdo (1851–1942) for his book *Wren's City Churches*, published in 1883. The floral designs of William Morris and the Arts and Crafts Movement were also influential in formulating the Art Nouveau look.

The first buildings to be influenced by Art Nouveau appeared at the end of the 1880s. Although the United States never entered the mainstream of the Art Nouveau style, the spiky floral decorations for the 4,000-seat Chicago Auditorium in 1889 by Louis Sullivan (1856–1924) showed that the look had crossed the Atlantic even then.

It was in the fast-expanding Belgian capital of Brussels, through the works of Victor Horta (1861–1947), that an architectural style began to evolve. Horta's Hotel Tassel, designed in 1892, featured exposed floral ironwork and used linear tendril decoration on both walls and ceilings.

Having mastered the 'whiplash' line, Horta applied it extensively – notably in staircases – in buildings such as the Hotel Solvay (1894) and the Maison and Atelier Horta (1898–1900). At the same time, his structural and exterior design became increasingly adventurous. The Maison du Peuple of 1897 balanced the elements of interlaced ironwork and elliptical windows in a sweeping concave façade. Horta's 'A l'Innovation' department store in 1901 was even more dramatic, presenting a soaring vertical composition of glass and curved ironwork to the street.

Another Belgian, Henri van de Velde (1863–1957), first experimented with the Art Nouveau style through typography and book decoration. He progressed to interior decoration with the Hotel Otlet in 1894, and a year later built his own house at Bloemenwerf near Uccle. In marked contrast to Horta's flamboyant townhouses, it incorporated Art Nouveau lines into a rural idiom with striped gables and shuttered windows.

Van de Velde went on to design interiors for Bing's Paris shop before moving to Germany. There he set up the Weimar School of Arts and Crafts, which subsequently became the Bauhaus.

France also had one radical thinker in the shape of the

theorist Eugène Viollet-le-Duc (1814–79), who proposed a new 'rationalist' approach to architecture based upon rediscovering Gothic principles of constructing ribbed vaults, only using iron. Viollet-le-Duc went against the establishment view in preaching that iron should be used 'honestly', and left exposed, rather than hiding it with terracotta and other fake masonry.

His theories were to prove particularly influential to French architects of Art Nouveau. Of these, the greatest exponent was Hector Guimard (1867–1942), who designed the entrances for the Paris Mètro system as well as a number of prominent houses. His Castel Béranger, finished in 1898, deployed floral motifs quite reminiscent of Horta, and indeed followed a visit to Belgium. Unlike Horta, however, Guimard worked in cast as well as wrought-iron, and it was the former that provided the basic material for the numerous Métro entrances and ticket offices he designed from 1900.

Aside from Guimard and his contemporaries working in Paris, France had a second school of Art Nouveau architects working at Nancy in eastern France, at a colony led by the glassmaker Emile Gallé. Its outstanding achievement was the Villa Majorelle of 1900, which was designed chiefly by Henri Sauvage.

In both Belgium and France, there were a number of architects working along similar lines, and Art Nouveau could lay claim to being a movement of sorts. In Spain, Antoni Gaudi (1852–1926) worked in virtual isolation, and his only direct influences came from reading the works of Viollet-le-Duc, Ruskin and others. Yet Gaudi was arguably the most original of all Art Nouveau architects.

Born in Tarragona, Gaudi moved to Barcelona, the capital of Catalonia, around 1869, where he was influenced by traditional Moorish and Moroccan styles, and by a mission to create a new Catalan architecture. His buildings were consequently more exotic than those of his contemporaries.

There is one other fiercely individual architect of this period whose name is often associated with Art Nouveau. Charles Rennie Mackintosh (1858–1928) built almost exclusively in and around the city of Glasgow, where he had studied at the art school.

Mackintosh's first important commission came in 1896, when he won a competition to design a new School of Art for the city. At first sight, the building which he constructed over 12 years bears little resemblance to Art Nouveau works elsewhere. But the influence of Horta and Guimard can be detected in the general asymmetry, in the sparing use of elliptical curves, and in the delicate ironwork seen in the decorative brackets set against the studio windows.

The work of the Spanish architect Antoni Gaudi displays an eccentric fantastic use of stone that anticipates the organic qualities of concrete and plastic. Gaudi was profoundly religious, inspired by the forces of nature and by the Middle Ages.

ABOVE Casa Mila, Barcelona (1905–10). Also known as "La Pedrera", this apartment building has a rippling stone facade which gives the impression of molten lava. Inside, the plan is irregular; no two rooms are alike and all are many-sided and without right-angles. The balconies are ironwork and spiky in form; the windows have rounded corners.

ABOVE Casa Battló, Barcelona (1905–7). The sinuous shape of the stone dressings on the lower part of the building is repeated in the curved metal balustrades. Around the windows are pieces of coloured glass embedded in the wall.

■ frank lloyd wright: the early days

Frank Lloyd Wright (1867–1959) designed many buildings over a period of more than 60 years, from small modular houses, suburban palaces and factories, to churches and art galleries. His work is particularly important because of its influence on other architects practising throughout the twentieth century. His genius sprang not just from his ability to design buildings that were pleasing to the eye and to the environment, nor from his ability to create an interesting interior ground plan, but predominantly from his intuitive skill in combining all these elements into organically unified buildings.

Wright set up a studio 1889 in Oak Park, a wealthy suburb of Chicago, and spent much of the next 15 years designing and developing Prairie Style houses, many for patrons who lived in the immediate vicinity. The term 'Prairie' is derived from one of two designs that he had published in 1901 in the *Ladies' Home Journal* entitled 'A Home in a Prairie Town'. (The other design was called 'A Small House with Lots of Room in it'.) This design reveals many of the hallmarks that typify Wright's Prairie Style houses of this period – an asymmetrical ground-plan, a façade that reflects the arrangements of the rooms within, strong horizontal elements, shallow roofs with overhanging eaves and many screen-like windows. Inside, the focal point of the house is undoubtedly the fireplace, with strong axial lines running across the house. Above all, the house is designed to be lived in: from the built-in furniture to the deep eaves for keeping the house cool, the house is supremely practical.

The Ward Willitts house (1902) is situated in Highland Park on the outskirts of Chicago and displays many of the Prairie Style characteristics but blended with strong Japanese overtones. Like much of Wright's work during this period, the house is devoid of unnecessary ornament, with strong grid-like black-and-white facades which are not uncomfortable in the surrounding area. The basement, so prevalent in American suburban houses, has been raised out of the ground, creating a podium for the floors above. Many years later Wright attempted to analyse his guiding beliefs behind the designs of these early houses and, above all else, he deemed unity – both in relation to interior spaces and in relation to the house and its environment – a prime objective.

One of the strongest examples of Wright's Prairie Style is the house he designed for a businessman called Frederick C. Robie in 1907. Situated in a relatively built-up area of Chicago, the house occupies a tight corner site. Wright's solution was to impose one giant slab of the building on top (but shifted across) of another; the top slab housed the living rooms out of sight from passers-by, whereas the lower slab housed the children's playroom and the billiards room. The longitudinal thrust of the house is further emphasized by extended overhangs on the outside

(supported by a steel beam at one point), and by an open and flowing living space (combining the living and dining rooms) on the inside. Whereas earlier Wright houses may have incorporated somewhat 'relaxed' ground-plans, the Robie House manifested a complete departure from more formalized arrangements.

In addition to his predominantly domestic commissions, Wright received several other offers of work during this period, including the opportunity to design a church complex in his own neighbourhood of Oak Park, Chicago (1906). He managed to convince his patrons, the Unitarians, to abandon the traditional basilica plan and, in its place, he created a squarish meeting-hall. Like many of Wright's buildings, his brilliance in manipulating space within this church and the attached meeting area is hard to appreciate without actually standing within them. The design is based on squares and rectangles, a formula that is carried throughout the building, including the light fittings. Most important, however, is Wright's use of concrete on the exterior of the building, which is surfaced with a pebble aggregate. Such an unashamed use of this material was very unusual for works of architecture as opposed to engineering, and looks forward to the next decade.

ABOVE LEFT Interior of Unity Church, Oak Park, Chicago (Frank Lloyd Wright, 1906). Wright designed the interiors, including furniture and light fittings, for many of his buildings.

ABOVE The Ward Willitts house, Highland Park, Illinois (Frank Lloyd Wright, 1902). The bold geometry of this façade, created by wooden beams breaking the white paintwork, bears witness to Wright's interest in Japanese architecture. He used stained glass in many of his early houses to create coloured light effects inside.

RIGHT Unity Church, Oak Park, Chicago (Wright, 1906). The building was made primarily of concrete and coated with a special pebble aggregate. The primitive South-American inspired ornament is integral to the building.

■ progressive use of steel

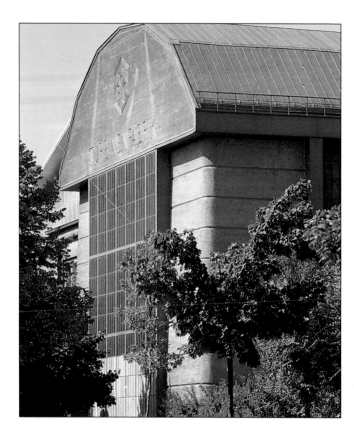

While the Americans developed the steel frame, and the English built their first tentative steel buildings, the Europeans, in the early years of this century, were taking the first steps towards the creation of a new architecture. A faith in the new technologies was a cornerstone of the new Modern movement. Steel and concrete were to be enjoyed for their own sakes. The cloaking of a steel frame in traditional stonework was seen as a crime.

First, however, the tenuous forms of Art Nouveau provided inspiration. The curvaceous steel of Victor Horta's (1861–1947) buildings in Brussels, Charles Rennie Mackintosh's (1868–1928) in Glasgow and H. Guimard's (1867–1943) Paris Métro stations had their moment of glory before the world of fantasy gave way to the puritan seriousness of the Modern movement.

The Dutch architect Hendrick Berlage's (1856–1934) Amsterdam Stock Exchange, completed in 1903, has exposed steel trusses in an expensive, sophisticated space. Berlage's passionate belief in revealing materials and construction led him to display the trusses as they were – undecorated and uncovered. As roofs do not need fireproofing, the trusses did not need to be clad in another material.

Peter Behrens' (1868–1940) Turbine House (1909) for A.E.G. on Berlin's Huttenstrasse is a first on many counts. The city had known steel structures before – overhead railways, factory roofs, the glasshouses at Dahlem – but it is at the A.E.G. Turbine House that exposed steel is at last

ABOVE LEFT A.E.G. Factory, Berlin, Germany (1909). Behrens started his career as an exponent of Art Nouveau. By the time he had been appointed as architect to the electrical firm of AEG, he had thrown off all decorative detailing and in this turbine factory he used poured concrete and steel more frankly than before except in pure engineering. His natural feeling for form gives the impression that he would be a master in any style.

ABOVE Tugendhat House, Brno, Czechoslovakia (Mies van der Rohe, 1930). This influential house pioneered the "open plan". The outside of the house demonstrates the simple geometry of the structure with large cantilevers and floor-to-ceiling windows. Mies liked to create a rectangular envelope in which screen walls provided strictly non-load-bearing, and often movable, partitions.

ABOVE RIGHT Fagus Works, Alfeld-an-der-Leine (Walter Gropius, 1911). One of the first truly modern buildings, the Fagus Works was essentially a cubic block incorporating glass curtain-walling that extended around the corners with no need for additional support.

reverently treated by a major architect. Although large, the building is single-storey. As it is generally assumed that single-storey buildings do not need fireproofing, Behrens was able to expose the steel. The rivets, the glazing bars and the hinged bases to the frames are all treated confidently, expressing the material. The massive concrete corners, however, are a reminder of masonry construction.

Behrens' pupil, Walter Gropius (1883–1969), took the next step with the Fagus Shoe Last Factory (1911) at Alfeld-an-der-Leine, where the corners of the building are all glass. Gropius said of the steel-framed building, "the role of the walls becomes restricted to that of mere screens, stretched between the upright columns of the frame to keep out rain, cold and noise".

The heyday of this International Style was marked by a preference for smooth white buildings. Concrete could give this, steel could not; many important modern buildings were framed in steel, and the structure and skin were then plastered over to look like concrete. For an architectural movement dedicated to truth to materials, this development was decidedly odd.

Arthur Korn and Ludwig Mies van der Rohe (1886–1969) broke away from the confines of the International Style to explore the possibilities of expressing the steel structure. Mies' 1929 Barcelona Pavilion and his Tugendhat House (1930) in Brno, Czechoslovakia, used cross-shaped columns and sheathed them in chromium-plated steel to emphasize the luxurious qualities of the material.

Arthur Korn's Fromm Rubber factory (1930) at Kopernick deserves a key place among the heroic buildings of the Modern movement. Constructed of red-painted steel with white glazed brick infill, it is the first building to express the steel frame as a regular cage. With this building, the architectural expression of multistorey steel structure had gone as far as it could go until the acceptance of welding.

During World War II, the structural steel industry in America was compelled to build big and fast. The construction of plants like Henry Kaiser's Fontana and Willow Run were miracles of speed and organization. However, at the end of the war, it was a small domestic building that acted as a revelation to architects and designers the world over.

In 1947, the West Coast Magazine *Arts and Architecture* commissioned Charles and Ray Eames, the designers of Eames furniture, to design a case study house for their own use. The Eames House uses steel with ease and lightness. All the elements – frame, decking and windows – are standard products out of catalogues. The lightness is achieved by taking the skin to the eaves over the fascia beam, by taking horizontal forces on clearly expressed diagonals and by using the same bar-joists as were later used in the Hertfordshire schools in England. The first domestic building to really express steel, the Eames House is one of the most cheerful houses of the Modern movement.

■ functionalism and De Stijl

The end of a century brings with it endless speculation, as if the change from one century to the next exercises some potent influence. Unfortunately, historical periods resist such convenient pigeonholing. The first stirring of what is called International Modern were in the 1880s, a time when artistic reaction to High Victorianism combined with advances in technology. Socially, however, the nineteenth century can be said to have met its conclusive end in the nightmare of World War I. After that, everything changed.

If Modernism in architecture conjures up a picture, it is the white Cubist style which developed in Germany and Austria in the early 1900s, spreading to Holland in the movement known as De Stijl, before reaching the rest of Europe and the United States.

De Stijl magazine – the title means 'The Style' – was founded in 1917. The name comprised a like-minded group of confident – if not arrogant – painters, sculptors and architects who loosely believed in the application of geometric abstraction. Piet Mondrian was one of the earliest to exploit the potential of geometric abstract images that relied on pure colour and form. However, it was notably J.J.P. Oud, Theo van Doesburg and Gerrit Rietveld who translated this idea into three dimensions.

Holland was not directly involved in World War I and, as a consequence, its architects were able to put contemporary ideas on modern architecture into practice well before many other countries. Oud's (1890–1963) design for seaside housing (1917) is an early example of clear, geometric forms, devoid of ornamentation. However, the design is still rigidly symmetrical. Oud, like many of his contemporaries was greatly influenced by H.P. Berlage, particularly in his 'honest' approach to structure and materials. Oud's housing at the Hook of Holland (1924–7) is so puritanical and uncluttered that it appears almost bland.

"Functionalism" was the word. "Form follows function", not the reverse as before. The past was despised – tradition, vernacular, ornament, the Beaux Arts School – all not only unnecessary in the new world but positively dishonest. But hadn't something like this been heard before? It was William Morris who had said it, and though his designs were different to look at, the reasoning of the two schools was similar in the moral purpose.

In 1923 van Doesburg presented plans and a model for a house which crystallized the De Stijl philosophy, but it was Rietveld's house for Mrs Schroeder (1923–4) that put the theories into practice. Influenced by Wright's use of asymmetrical plans in his Prairie Style houses, the Schroeder house appears to be constructed out of overlapping and intersecting two-dimensional planes that enclose three-dimensional space. The white and grey walls of the exterior are cut and highlighted by the graphic lines of the balcony railings and the window mullions which are painted red, blue, yellow and black. The distribution of wall to window space is approximately equal, so that the solidity

ABOVE Housing scheme, Hook of Holland (J.J.P. Oud, 1924–27). This scheme comprised two terraces of cheap housing with shops at the end of each block. The apparent simplicity of the houses with their white-painted rendered façades and horizontal bands of windows looks forward to the full-blown International Style.

LEFT Juliana School, Hilversum, Holland (1923). Marinus Dudok (1884–1974). In contrast with the International Modernism of Rietveld, Dudok cannot be easily categorized. He was a designer with a very personal treatment of roof, wall and glazing in which asymmetrical elements are combined with force and subtlety.

of construction is undermined by the sheer volume of openings. Inside, the abstract geometric theme is maintained throughout. By abolishing all the traditional signs by which a building is 'read' and understood Rietveld created a blueprint with endless possibilities.

Influenced by both the early Dutch Expressionists and the architecture of the De Stijl group, were the architects Willem Dudok (1884–1974) and Johannes Duiker (1890–1935). In Dudok's work, notably the Juliana school at Hilversum (1923), can be seen the reduction to structural essentials and the asymmetricality of Modernist design, but the use of 'warm' materials such as red brick and of deeply pitched roofs are strikingly individualistic. Duiker's commitment to the 'International Style' of the Modern movement was more profound. His buildings such as the Zonnestraal Sanatorium, Hilversum (1926–8, with Bijvoet) and the Open Air School in Amsterdam (1930–32) with their curtain-wall fenestration and white concrete, look to the Bauhaus.

ABOVE Open Air School, Amsterdam (1930–32). Johannes Duiker (1890–1935). Another member of the De Stijl group. This functional treatment of white concrete with simple fenestration remained internationally influential until after World War II.

RIGHT Bauhaus Buildings, Dessau, Germany (Gropius, 1926). In 1925 Gropius was commissioned to remodel the Bauhaus and become its principal. He was also commissioned to design a number of houses for the teaching staff. The result was a milestone in design-teaching, for the school was a combination of craft workshop and fine-art studio with architecture as the link. The classroom block is in simple black and white, the precursor of many post-war schools all over Europe. The workshops are noticeably more industrial particularly in their window treatment. The square-panelled metal windows are typical of mass-produced industrial units.

■ the bauhaus

To some extent, the seeds of the Bauhaus had been planted before the war by the Werkbund, an association set up in 1907 at the prompting of Hermann Muthesius (1861–1927) with the dual aim of improving the quality of manufactured goods and promoting the role of designers in industry. Among the designers involved in the Werkbund was the Belgian Henri van de Velde, who set up a school of arts and crafts in Weimar. This school provided the premises and some of the staff for the Bauhaus.

Walter Gropius (1883–1969) was chosen as director from

a list supplied by van de Velde. In his opening proclamation, Gropius urged the breaking down of barriers between artists and craftsmen, at the same time stating unequivocally: "The ultimate aim of all creative activity is the building."

The Bauhaus was set up as a series of workshops and in its initial form was inspired by an admiration for Britain's Arts and Crafts Movement. Among the initial teachers were such renowned artists as Johannes Itten and Lionel Feininger, later joined by Paul Klee and Wassily Kandinsky.

All students had to take a generalized *Vorkurs*, taught by Itten, which in many ways was a prototype for the foundation course taken by many art students today. The workshops were intended to produce designs that could be sold to industry, but achieved little success in the early years.

Gropius, meanwhile, retained his architectural practice together with his partner Adolf Meyer, and in 1921 they were commissioned to build a villa for the industrialist Adolf Sommerfeld. The Sommerfeld Haus provided the first opportunity for Bauhaus students to become involved in designing for a real building, and they produced the interiors, fittings and furniture. Constructed entirely from wood, it resembled a log cabin in the traditional *Heimatstil*, and was adorned with Expressionist wood carvings and stained glass. Expressionism was on the way out in Germany, however, to be replaced by a more rational style known as Neue Sachlichkeit – New Objectivity.

The following year, 1922, the Bauhaus changed direction, turning away from Arts and Crafts towards machines and technology. Itten left and was replaced by the Hungarian László Moholy-Nagy, while Gropius revised many of his original ideas under the influence of the Dutch Abstract Cubist Theo van Doesburg.

In 1923 the Bauhaus put on its first important exhibition at which the central exhibit was an experimental house designed by the painter Georg Muche. The Haus am Horn was one of the first prototypes for a house that could be made from mass-produced components. Its simple structure consisted of a square frame of steel and concrete with a clerestory-lit central living room surrounded by the other rooms. The prevailing spirit was of functionality, with each room built to fulfil a single purpose, and Marcel Breuer's (1902–81) kitchen was especially prophetic, making use of a continuous work surface with cupboards suspended above and below.

In 1925, growing nationalist hostility forced the Bauhaus to leave Weimar. Gropius found a new location in the industrial city of Dessau, where sufficient financial support was provided to construct a complex of buildings to house the school. The Bauhaus at Dessau consisted of two blocks linked by an enclosed bridge, housing lecture rooms, workshops, student accommodation, a refectory, a theatre, a gymnasium and Gropius and Meyer's architectural practice. The skeleton was of reinforced concrete, while one side of the workshops consisted of a glass curtain wall, and the roof was flat, covered by a new waterproof material.

Like the Haus am Horn, the new buildings were striking by their adherence to functionality and by the absence of decoration.

Gropius left the Bauhaus in 1928 to concentrate on his own practice and was succeeded by Hannes Meyer, who immediately set the Bauhaus on a new course of social responsibility. Eclectic tastes were dropped in favour of design for the masses, with the intention of producing inexpensive items such as plywood furniture that could be afforded by working people.

Under Meyer, the Bauhaus thrived economically, but growing political pressures forced his resignation after just two years. Mies van der Rohe (1886–1969), already an accomplished technician in steel and glass, took over. He introduced a greater emphasis on architectural theory, and concentrated once more on producing exclusive designs for a wealthy élite. Despite Mies' attempts to keep politics out of the Bauhaus, it was closed by the government in 1932 and the buildings were ransacked by the Nazis. A final attempt to revive the Bauhaus in a disused Berlin factory came to an abrupt end when it was raided by police and the Bauhaus was closed for good.

In the following years, Gropius, Mies van der Rohe, Moholy-Nagy and Breuer were among those who joined the exodus of artists and intellectuals from Nazi Germany to the United States. There, they achieved influential positions and disseminated the ideas of the Bauhaus, with Moholy-Nagy even going so far as to create a 'New Bauhaus' in Chicago in 1937. Mies van der Rohe became Dean of Architecture at the Illinois Institute of Technology, while Gropius took the Chair of Architecture at Harvard, and both were instrumental in ensuring the long-overdue acceptance of Modernism by the American establishment.

ABOVE The third in a series of housing projects Gropius undertook after leaving the Bauhaus, Siemensstadt was a development of low-cost flats fitted with modern conveniences, constructed with the techniques of prefabrication Gropius had pioneered at Dessau.

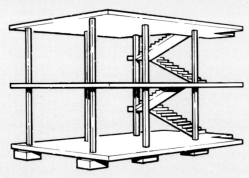

TOP German Pavilion for the Barcelona Exhibition (reconstruction) (Mies van der Rohe, 1929). With Mies van der Rohe, the second phase of the Modern movement began. Like the De Stijl group, the basic abstract foundation is apparent, but now infinitely more sophisticated. The extreme simplicity is deceptive: each element has been calculated with immense attention and to the highest standard.

ABOVE the standard plan for the "Dom-ino" houses of Le Corbusier, devised in 1914, was a revelation to architects the world over. The proposal was to divorce the basic framework of a house from the demands of the internal arrangement: the reinforced concrete frame simply carried the floors and stairs.

■ miles van der rohe and le corbusier

It was in Germany and France that the two great masters of the Modern movement were born — Ludwig Mies van der Rohe (1886–1969) and Charles-Edouard Jeanneret (1887–1966), self-styled Le Corbusier.

Mies and Le Corbusier were radically opposed in temperament and outlook, however committed both were in principle to the new architecture. Of the two, Le Corbusier had, at least at first, the greater influence. This was due in a large part to indefatigable self promotion through his publications. Mies on the other hand set out deliberately to suppress personality and produce a refined architecture of reduction, perfectly expressed in his famous remark "Less is more". His other guiding maxim was "Reason is the first principle of·all human work", a saying he discovered in the writings of St Thomas Aquinas. In his architecture the form *is* the structure; he never tried to force structure into a preconceived form.

This eventually led to some extremes of structural expression, hard to justify under any grounds other than sheer aesthetics; nevertheless his unswerving consistency of purpose has been one of the most impressive contributions to twentieth-century architecture.

ABOVE Villa Savoye, Poissy France (Le Corbusier, 1928–31). Villa Savoye is one of the private houses Corbusier built in and around Paris: these have had an immense influence on modern architects. This house displays all the features most associated with Corbusier's work. The roof terrace is treated as a space in its own right; the main floor is raised on pillars (*pilotis*) so that the garden can extend under the house; the windows are treated as horizontal strips. This formal, even classical style owes a lot to the particular qualities of reinforced concrete.

► early works of le corbusier

As a young architect Le Corbusier (1887–1965) was fortunate enough to work in the offices of both Auguste Perret and Peter Behrens. From the former he was able to comprehend the possibilities of reinforced concrete; from the latter he was able to learn the positive implications of combining design with large-scale mechanization. Both themes came together in his "Dom-ino" housing scheme (1914–15) with which he hoped to provide quick, cheap dwellings. Designed as a kit, each unit consisted of a six-pillared reinforced concrete frame which supported cantilevered slabs of reinforced concrete. The 'bare bones' design based on strict geometric principles and flexible in the manner in which the building could be subdivided, highlighted his preoccupation with creating a new basic system of construction. The walls no longer carried any weight so that they could be placed anywhere.

Together with his friend Amédée Ozenfant (1886–1966), Le Corbusier set up a magazine entitled *L'Esprit Nouveau* which underlined the need for a new architecture in tune with the developments of the machine age. While Le Corbusier was uninspired by buildings of the immediate past, he certainly admired architecure of Classical antiquity and believed wholeheartedly in the notion that there existed inherent forms of beauty. A selection of articles taken from the magazine were published in book form under the title *Vers une architecture* (1923), which proved to be one of the most significant architectural publications of the twentieth century.

Le Corbusier's sketches for the Maison Citrohan (1919–22) reveals the hallmarks of his own style – a geometric white block constructed out of concrete, raised on slender columns (*pilotis*), a flat roof, and lots of windows set flush with the wall and terraces. Each element of the house has been reduced to its bare functional essentials, geometrically expressed – thus it has become (in Le Corbusier's much-quoted phrase) a 'machine for living in'.

The Villa Savoye at Poissy (1928–9) neatly summarizes Le Corbusier's self-proclaimed 'Five Points of a New Architecture' – a free plan, a free façade, *pilotis*, a terrace and ribbon windows. While appearing to implement his machine-inspired ideas, it also reveals a sculptural treatment of forms, an element of his work that became more pronounced as he grew older.

Having established his reputation with a number of domestic commissions, Le Corbusier turned his attentions to large-scale projects, not least of which was his plans for the Ville Radieuse ('Shining City'). He also submitted a number of plans for competitions including those for the Palace of the League of Nations (1927) and for the Palace of the Soviets (1931). The latter included an enormous assembly hall with a roof suspended from a giant parabolic arch. Successful projects included the Maison de Refuge, Paris (1930–3), a large building with a ship-like presence, one wall of which was almost entirely glass.

◼ international modern

LEFT Lovell Beach House, Newport Beach, California, USA (1926). R.M. Schindler (1887–1953). Born in Vienna, Schindler was taught there by Otto Wagner before moving to the USA, where his practice was principally domestic. This example shows his dexterity in handling concrete.

RIGHT House, Grunewald, Germany (Mendelsohn, 1929). International Style house, in a garden setting. This German example is typical of the architecture many refugees brought with them to England and the USA during the years before World War II.

LEFT Melnikov's House, Moscow (1927). Konstantin Melnikov (1890–1974). A rare survival from the brief period of Russian Modernism before the Stalin era. This house was the architect's own and is made up of two cylindrical sections linked by a staircase.

RIGHT Steiner House, Vienna (1910). Loos was the hard-line architect of the Modern movement, to whom ornament was a "crime". His influence can be gauged by the fact that these houses at the time highly revolutionary, now look merely "modern".

ABOVE The Walter Dodge house, Los Angeles, California, (Irving Gill, 1915–16), demolished. Gill's proto- Modernist style featured smooth stucco walls with large windows and little decorative detailing.

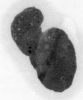

■ art deco

The term 'Art Deco' was popularized in the 1960s and is used to describe a largely decorative style (roughly 1920–1940) which is characterized by strong geometric forms, striking colours and graphic sharpness. Named after the Paris Exposition Internationale des Arts Décoratifs et Industriels Modernes (1925), it was this exhibition that provided the first large-scale showcase of the decorative arts and architecture in a 'moderne' style.

It can be argued that Art Moderne was purely the commercial interpretation of Modernism; the two movements certainly shared common influences such as Cubist, Abstract and Expressionist art, the architecture of the Arts and Crafts practitioners, Frank Lloyd Wright and the Secessionists. The Kärntner Bar in Vienna, designed by Adolf Loos in 1907, appears to foresee both Modernism and Art Moderne. Similarly, Le Corbusier's *L'Esprit Nouveau* pavilion at the Exposition was an inspiration to all manner of architects. While Art Moderne and Art Deco were decorative, Modernism was exclusive and rarefied, and above all, hard on eyes accustomed to more ornamental and traditional forms of architecture. Art Deco, on the other hand, combined the solid geometric shapes thought of at the time as decidedly "modern" but was mellowed with sculptural ornament, metalwork and colour.

The Exposition highlighted Paris as the centre of the Art Deco style. The grand Art Deco entrance to the Exposition, the 'Porte d'Honneur', with extensive decorative metalwork by Edgar Brandt, blatantly announced it to the world. Within, Robert Mallet-Steven's 'Pavilion du Tourisme' personified the more Modernist tendencies of Art Moderne whereas the furniture designer's Emile-Jacques Ruhlmann's 'Hôtel d'un Collectionneur', designed by the architect Pierre Patout, displayed a more restrained Classical form of Art Deco. However, the Exposition by its very nature was not only international – pavilions representing many countries betrayed "modern" sentiments – but also temporary.

In the years following the Exposition, commercial Art Moderne, or Art Deco, appeared throughout Europe and the United States. In France itself, Art Deco is distinct for its restrained reductivist façades, lightened with floral and figurative ironwork and sculpture. In Britain the two styles were used frequently for the many hundreds of cinemas that were sprouting up throughout the country; the façade of the Leicester Square Odeon in London is a particularly fine example of Art Moderne and is sheathed in shiny black cladding. London Underground, which underwent an extensive expansion in the 1920s and 1930s, built many stations in a much more understated Modernist Art Moderne.

The country in which Art Deco and Moderne architecture really blossomed was the United States. Generously fed on the home-grown Modernist ideas of Frank Lloyd Wright, and eager to employ styles of architecture devoid of overt historical and cultural associations, the United States took to Art Deco enthusiastically. The style was adopted not only

ABOVE Apartment block, Ealing, London, 1930s. Muted Art Moderne was often used for the vast quantity of speculative building that went up in Britain between the wars. Green roof tiles are peculiar to this period of architecture and were sometimes adopted for 'Spanish hacienda' style housing.

LEFT Hoover factory, Perivale, London (Wallis Gilbert and Partners, 1932–8). Egyptian influences are easily discernible in this spectacular palace of industry.

FAR LEFT Chrysler Building, New York (William van Alen, 1928–30). Like many of the skyscrapers being built in Manhattan at this time, the Chrysler building was a vertical "city" of offices with its many elevators serving as the main routes of communication.

for large-scale structures such as New York skyscrapers and Miami Beach apartment blocks, but also small buildings such as diners. Often clad in a skin of stainless steel, American diners embody the impact of 'streamlining' (the adulation of machine and car technology and styling), an important element of Art Deco style.

Skyscrapers, such as the Chrysler Building by William van Alen (1928–30) were the pinnacle of Art Deco achievement. A soaring testament to corporate acceptance, these skyscrapers dominated Manhattan architecture in particular during the late 1920s and through the 1930s, and they included the Chanin Building (Sloan & Robertson, 1929), the Empire State Building (Shreve, Lamb & Harmon, 1930–1), the McGraw-Hill Building (Raymond Hood, 1930–1) and the Rockefeller Center (Raymond Hood and others, 1931–9).

■ style after world war II

A FTER THE WAR, new socialist and democratic governments in both Europe and the United States oversaw the development of wide-scale social welfare, promising protection "from the cradle to the grave" with improved housing, education and health facilities. Such good intentions obviously necessitated massive state building – houses, schools, universities and hospitals were needed, and fast. Local authorities with limited funds at their disposal and large numbers of people to care for seized on Modernism because it was not only a new style of architecture for a new style of government, but it was also fundamentally cheaper to build.

Under such patronage, Modernism thrived throughout the 1950s and 1960s, and developed into two very distinct styles. The first used concrete as a sculptural medium and its sheer strength can be seen when Le Corbusier used it to dramatic effect at Notre Dame du Haut, Ronchamp, France (1950–55). This style of Modernism was generally used for large-scale public buildings (for mainly privately funded works). It could be argued that some of Frank Lloyd Wright's structures of this period, such as the Guggenheim Museum in New York (1943–59), are fundamentally Modernist in approach although he preferred to stay one step removed from European Modernism.

The second style of Modernism relied on steel and glass for a harder, more rigid appearance and its chief exponent, Mies van der Rohe, used the Farnsworth House in Fox River, Illinois (1945–51) as a précis of this form of steel and glass construction. Throughout this period, it was used extensively for office buildings in particular. At the same time, experimental architects such as Buckminster Fuller and Bruce Goff designed buildings in the United States that turned their backs resolutely on the 'four walls and a roof' concept of architecture, producing wonderfully individualist works.

The idea of separating home life from work, zoning, and of moving housing out of the centre of cities, combined with the post-war population explosion, resulted in numerous schemes for new towns and "projects".

Unfortunately, governments were so desperate to rebuild quickly that many opportunities were wasted and minimum-standard housing, haphazardly sited, became the reality, rather than well-thought-out schemes providing quality housing that would have taken longer to realize yet would have been better in the long term.

In the United States, this rush to build resulted in vast stretches of prefabricated "tract" housing, such as Levittown on Long Island – a 17,500 house development by William Levitt, who pioneered the mass-produced assembly-line approach to house building called 'site fabrication'.

Britain's planners tackled the demand for housing, particularly in the south, by building from 1949 twelve new towns, eight of which were around London – Stevenage, Harlow, Welwyn Garden City, Hatfield, Hemel Hempstead, Bracknell, Crawley and Basildon.

There was a spate of new university building, notably in Britain, where the number of universities more than doubled as the government sought belatedly to catch up with the educational achievements of other Western countries. Art galleries, concert halls, opera houses and theatres also sprang up in profusion throughout the prosperous United States and to a lesser extent, across Europe.

Le Corbusier's 1947 Unité d'Habitation project at Marseilles although a housing scheme, was to prove the source of a new aesthetic that became embedded in many 1950s and 1960s public developments.

The walls of the Unité were of *béton brut* – raw concrete that displayed the texture of the shuttering used in the forming process. Critics coined the word 'Brutalist' to denote Le Corbusier's assertion of his material and its expressive qualities.

Brutalism became largely synonymous with the use of massive slabs of concrete through such developments as London's South Bank arts complex and the shopping centre at Cumbernauld – a new town built near Glasgow, once seen as a brave new world and now derelict.

■ frank lloyd wright assessed

Architecture is of all arts the most arrogant. It is publicly inescapable and there is no essential correlation between form and function. In spite of William Morris and Walter Gropius, buildings can be functionally artificial, even callous – witness Blenheim Palace – yet remain great architecture. Le Corbusier, in the Unité, was only doing what other architects had done for centuries; that was to provide buildings to which the inhabitants would have to adapt, the opposite of humanist ideals where there was tenant participation.

The rationale was infectious. In the book *The Modern Flat* by F.R.S. Yorke and Frederick Gibberd (1937), Le Corbusian theories are argued with great plausibility. In it there is an aerial photograph of a typical speculator's suburb,

encroaching like a predator to devour the surrounding countryside. Underneath is an anglicized Unité block, standing in parkland studded with lakes and woods. You are invited to choose which is to be preferred – the ugly sprawl, profligate of land, or the orderly town in the air surrounded by green lawns salvaged by the site economy.

The proposition was doubtless oversimplified, but whether the reaction now is oversimplified, only time will tell. To be sure, Le Corbusier and his followers neglected the social side-effects of their doctrinal authoritarianism, yet the basic problem of land use remains unsolved and is more acute today than in the immediate post-war years.

In the United States, Mies was building flats too, with even greater arrogance and disregard for the tenants than his French contemporary. He built the twin block Lake Shore Drive flats on the Chicago waterfront. No balconies were allowed, they might break the geometry of the block, nor were curtains permitted which, subject to individual choice, would be bound to compromise the purity of his facades.

TOP Falling Water Bear Run, Pennsylvania, USA (Wright, 1937–39). One of the most extraordinary and exciting houses of the century. On a dramatic site above a waterfall in woodland, Wright created a concrete masterpiece to rival anything in this material attempted by his European contemporaries. On the waterfall side, two huge and opposed cantilevered balconies are suspended over the water. This cantilever theme extends all around the house; the concrete is

rendered a smooth white in contrast with the rough vertical elements in natural stone. The whole result is a complex, but at the same time harmonious sculptural composition.

ABOVE The interior view shows how the structural logic of white horizontal concrete and natural stone piers is integral throughout the house. Note Wright's favourite device of breaking up ceiling heights to create spatial interest and architectural decoration.

► wright and the guggenheim museum

One of the first important post-war projects to be undertaken in the United States was Frank Lloyd Wright's Guggenheim Museum in New York. From first designs in 1943, the Guggenheim was started in 1945 but only completed 14 years later, after a decade of impasse.

The finished building, while not entirely true to the original plans, was revolutionary as an art gallery. Instead of arranging the walls for pictures around a conventional rectangular interior, Wright devised a completely original space, an ascending spiral ramp that expanded as it climbed upwards.

It was the outcome of a preoccupation with ramps that Wright had nurtured for many years, and which had been manifested in previous designs ranging from a giant car park to a department store.

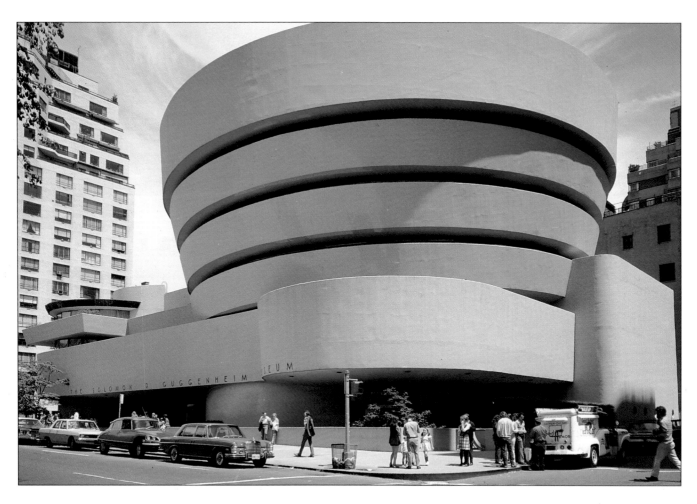

ABOVE LEFT David Wright House, Phoenix, Arizona, USA (1952). Wright built this desert house for his son, and based it on a circle theme. The entrance approach is up a helical ramp which serves the main rooms – curved on plan – situated on the upper level.

Indeed, it was not until a desperate tenant actually fried an egg in August behind his uncurtained window, that blinds – metallic faced and standard – were allowed by the management.

Compared with these architectural authoritarians, the equally authoritarian Frank Lloyd Wright now stands out as a model of humanity, diametrically opposed in principle to his European rivals. Wright believed in individual houses standing in one acre of land – an easy proposition for America in the fifties. At least his buildings were built for people to love and live in, close to the essential nature to which Wright felt they were entitled and on which they were dependent for spiritual wellbeing.

Wright, Mies and Le Corbusier pursued their own paths, gathering supporters but relatively careless of whether they were establishing schools to continue and propagate their theories. The truth is that such men are inimitable: one cannot become a Le Corbusier by designing to his Modulor, or a Mies by building in steel and glass. Possibly of the three, Wright's influence, because so profoundly individual, has been the least disastrous. Le Corbusier has something to answer for, he is behind every tower block in post-war Europe, and those who thought that Mies could be imitated on the cheap have been quickly disillusioned. His influence is in many of the tawdry-looking schools and factory units of our towns.

ABOVE Guggenheim Museum, New York (Frank Lloyd Wright, 1943–59). More like a multistorey carpark than a museum from its outward appearance, the Guggenheim's characteristic form has become a visual icon in its own right.

■ later works of le corbusier

One of the most influential exponents of the pre-war Modern Movement, Le Corbusier was commissioned to design mass-housing projects. His Unité d'Habitation project at Marseilles in France (1946–52) a block of 337 flats which included a school, shops, laundry and communal areas, is the greatest practical realization of Le Corbusier's principles. The apartments, which were to house 1,600 inhabitants, were designed according to 23 styles, varying from a large family unit to a simple studio flat. The project, and particularly his use of raw concrete (Le Corbusier's favoured medium), aroused wide controversy, yet he was to influence a generation of architects – as can be seen from numerous housing developments around Europe such as the Grands Ensembles in France and such Italian schemes as the Forte di Quezzi residential quarter in Genoa (built 1960).

Unfortunately, these followers did not always think through their plans to quite such a degree as Le Corbusier, with the result that the Modern Movement failed in the area which was most important to politicians and planners as well as architects – mass housing. Their predilection for impersonal high-rise blocks discredited the movement in the eyes of the public and alienated a generation, turning architects into bogeymen for many.

Projects such as the Roehampton Estate in London and the Park Hill and Hyde Park estates in Sheffield, while winning initial praise and awards, did not find favour with the people who actually had to live in them. They felt isolated and under threat in their flats. The very size of such projects were felt to be intimidating – particularly for people used to little "two up, two down" houses – and the

ABOVE Supreme Court, Chandigarh, Punjab (Le Corbusier, 1951–56). A building designed for the Indian climate, with *brise-soleils* and a canopy-like roof to give protection against both sun and monsoon.

BELOW Unité d'Habitation, Marseilles, France (Le Corbusier, 1947–52). One of the most influential buildings of the twentieth century. It incorporates the architect's dream of multistorey self-contained blocks of flats, standing in the midst of parkland.

LEFT Unité d'Habitation, Berlin, Germany (Le Corbusier, 1957). A third Unité (the second in Nantes, 1953) was built for the post-war Interbau exhibition. This model, backed up by Le Corbusier's own persuasive polemics, excited architects across the world. The result has spread worldwide.

ABOVE Carpenter Center for the Visual Arts, Harvard (Le Corbusier, 1960). Le Corbusier's individualistic style never attracted the popularity in America that it had in Europe.

walkways, or "streets in the sky", while intended to provide meeting places which could engender community feelings, replacing the old doorsteps or garden walls as gossip areas, soon became desolate and windy no-go areas frequented by muggers and packs of dogs.

'Brutalist' use of concrete showed itself in the United States, first, with Le Corbusier's Carpenter Visual Arts Center at Harvard, built in 1960, then with Paul Rudolph's Art and Architecture Building at Yale begun the following year.

The Carpenter, Le Corbusier's only building to be completed in the United States, employed many of his stock motifs, including a concrete grid framework and *brise soleils* (shade-making elements) and sat a little awkwardly alongside its predominantly red-brick neighbours at Harvard.

Rudolph's building at Yale, on the other hand, employed massive columns of textured, reinforced concrete in a labyrinthine composition of towers and terraces that anticipated some Brutalist developments in Britain.

later works of mies van der rohe

The steel architecture of Mies van der Rohe spread round the globe. The campus he designed for the Illinois Institute of Technology, most of which was built during the 1940s, was unified by a grid spread over the site. The buildings had black painted steel frames which fitted on the grid.

The design of exposed steel frame and brick infill dates from Arthur Korn's Kopernick factory, but in the intervening decade the all-welded structure had become feasible. This meant that the detailing at I.I.T. could be neater and waterproof joints could be made, enabling rolled sections to be built up and exposed on the outside of the building.

The Minerals and Metals Research Building (1943) was the first I.I.T. building to be completed and set the grammar of the structural frame which is expressed inside and out. The Library (1944) was the greatest of the I.I.T. designs, using the same design in a more sophisticated way. It has rolled sections joined by continuous welds to give members a complex profile, which hold the brick infill clear of the columns, emphasizing the direction of span.

The Alumni Memorial Hall (1946) was, however, the most influential of the I.I.T. buildings. As it is a two-storey building, Mies had to face the problem of fire protection. At that time, Chicago architects believed that technology would soon give them a fire-resistant steel and students designed buildings on the assumption that this already existed. Mies could not wait for this development, however, and the Alumni Hall went up with the structural steel encased in concrete. This fireproofing concrete was faced with steel which formed part of a light steel framework on the outside of the columns. Architectural purists were horrified; the details did lack the clarity of the Library, but at last a fireproof steel building had been built which looked like a steel building.

Mies van der Rohe had settled in Chicago, the home of steel construction, but it was in New York that his major corporate work was built. The Seagram Building which Mies van der Rohe designed with Philip Johnson (1954–8) is of crucial significance in the development of the office block; many hundreds of near copies were designed throughout the world in the following decades. The building was, in essence, the technical realization of Mies's glass tower of 35 years earlier, in that the basic structure was sheathed in glass with very little interruption of the silhouette. The building was set back from the road allowing a clear view from pedestrian level, and a horizontal slab indicated the entrance. Like all of Mies van der Rohe's buildings, quality craftsmanship was maintained throughout.

In Italy, Gio Ponti designed the elegant Pirelli Building in Milan (1957) which broke away from the Mies formula by incorporating bevelled sides, made possible by the double vertebrate system of construction. The 'glass and steel' block was used for a number of other purposes in addition to corporate offices during the 1950s, notably for the United Nations Building (1947–50) developed from an idea by Le Corbusier, the SAS Hotel in Copenhagen designed by Arne Jacobsen in 1958, and the New York State Theater, Lincoln Center, New York by Philip Johnson (1960).

FAR LEFT Seagram Building, New York (Ludwig Mies van der Rohe with Philip Johnson, 1954–8). Mies van der Rohe's scheme for a glass office block in 1921 could not have been more prophetic; at the time it was structurally inconceivable, but within 35 years the idea had become a practicality.

TOP AND ABOVE Farnsworth House, Fox River, Illinois, USA (Mies van der Rohe, 1950). In this country pavilion, Mies expressed and concentrated every aspect of his genius into a simple rectangular volume of steel and glass. It is a Classical house, Greek in subtlety and attention to detail, which floats serenely above its site on the eight columns which support roof and floor. A central core provides the bathroom, otherwise the plan is open, lightly screened into areas for sleeping and living. The walls of plate glass spill the interior into the surrounding trees. Furnishings are spare – not a house for the untidy.

ABOVE LEFT Apartments, Lake Shore Drive, Chicago, USA (Mies van der Rohe, 1948–51). Mies refused to allow balconies to these apartment buildings which he argued would betray their purity of form. Individual curtains were also banned: only standard metallic blinds were eventually permitted to screen these all-glass walls.

■ the new architecture of the 1960s

By the 1960s, the second phase of Modernism was over. The best of the young contemporaries had begun to throw off early allegiances and strike out on their own. The United States provided the most propitious field for the new postwar generation, and the attention of the architectural world was first directed there. The list is impressive: Skidmore, Owings & Merrill, Saarinen, Rudolph, Johnson, Pei, Kahn and many others.

The new architecture took fire in countries across the World – Japan, Australia, South America prominent among them. In Europe, the fifties and sixties saw the gradual establishment and acceptance, however grudging, of the Modern movement. Pockets of resistance hung on to older traditions. In England, Raymond Erith stoutly maintained his impeccable Classical convictions, dying a few years too soon to see his dedication recognized and his influence acknowledged and taken up again.

At another level of course, in all Western countries, a bastardized vernacular remained popular with the general public. In England, the respectably dull neo-Classicism of the 1930s declined into "Estates Georgian", with its fibreglass ornaments substituting for the old stone and plaster, or a kind of aerosol vernacular, with surface Elizabethan applied to the façade. Public housing, tied to liberal policies and hard-hearted economics, stayed with the high rise – quick and cheap to build. New towns followed a vaguely Scandinavian line, brick terraces with a scattering of stubby towers to make up required densities.

ABOVE City Hall, Boston, Massachusetts (Kallmann, McKinnell & Knowles, 1962–7). The architects successfully managed to combine a sense of civic authority and openness by creating a monumental building, but one that was "broken up" by means of perforations and a deep recess at ground level.

Events such as the partial collapse of the high-rise block Ronan Point in London in 1968 after a gas explosion hardly settled the public's collective mind and gradually authorities, which had previously been so keen to erect high-rise blocks and huge projects, found themselves demolishing the very same buildings – often before they had even finished paying for their construction.

One notable example was the Pruitt-Igoe project in St. Louis, Missouri. This was built between 1955 and 1958 to the design of Minoru Yamasaki (who also designed the World Trade Center in New York). Hailed as innovative at its conception, it was in 1972 blown up due to the campaigns of its residents.

An alternative to the unpopular large developments was the renewal of existing housing stock – which made great sense for cities such as New York, whose West Side area was full of sub-standard 'Brownstone' houses. One of the advantages of re-development was that communities did not need to be split up or relocated and could be consulted about their needs or desires.

The 1960s saw a curious restatement of Modernism manifested in the style known as New Brutalism. The Hunstanton School in Norfolk by Peter and Alison Smithson gave the movement its impetus in a building where everything was frankly exposed. Not only structure became part of form, but the services, the ducts, pipes and conduits

as well. A decade or so later this aesthetic became the more sophisticated "High Tech". Whatever its merits, High Tech is a genuinely new and individual style. It differs from Brutalism by a lightheartedness suggested by Pop Art and commercial styling: perhaps it is nearer the spirit of Art Deco than the pastiche of that style that re-emerged in the 1970s.

During the 1960s the "glass and steel" style was widely used for office blocks, but so too was a more architectonic sculptural style inspired by Le Corbusier's experiments with the plastic nature of concrete – particularly for organizations with the need to house varied activites. In Japan, Kunio Mayekawa designed the Kyoto Town Hall (1958–60) in which the raw concrete had the surface appearance of wood and where the construction was a powerful feature of the design.

Kenzo Tange was commissioned to design headquarters for the Yamanashi Press and Radio Company in Kofu (1964–7). Huge concrete service towers delineate the building at the same time as providing the struts from which hang the various working spaces, including broadcasting studios and shops. The building has the appearance of being put together from a kit (it looks as if floors can be added or subtracted as necessary) and its technical wizardry has obviously affected the design – a characteristic that was to be explored in the 1970s and 1980s.

The TWA terminal at Kennedy Airport, New York, designed by Eero Saarinen (1960) reveals a third, more expressive, sculptural approach. Massive curved planes sweep together, and flight is implied by the "wings" of the roof. The purpose and shape of the rooms within are of little consequence to the form and façade which dominate all.

The corporate "steel and glass" style reached its logical

TOP A failed experiment. By the early 1970s, authorities throughout the world found themselves blowing up high-rise blocks they had thought were the cure to all their housing ills.

ABOVE Falmer House, University of Sussex (Sir Basil Spence, 1962). The main building in the university complex, it is derivative of a fortified castle with central courtyard and moat.

conclusion with the Hancock Tower in Boston designed by the firm of I.M. Pei and Associates (architect H. Cobb) in 1969. Reflective glass provided a 'living' skin while the precision perfection of the steel mullion system provided the ultimate corporate slickness.

■ 1960s architecture of the United States

TOP LEFT Foreign Office, Brasilia, Brazil (1962–70). Oscar Niemeyer (b1907). This majestic building in the new capital city, Brasilia, shows Niemeyer in an unusually restrained, even Classical mood. A strong adherent of Le Corbusier, his employment of form is usually more romantic, even Expressionist.

TOP CENTRE Salk Institute, La Jolla, California, USA (Kahn, 1963–65). A severe but interestingly modelled group of buildings, reminiscent of Le Corbusier in its treatment of concrete. More subtle in detailing than may appear at first glance.

TOP RIGHT School of Art and Architecture, Yale, New Haven, USA (1963). Paul Rudolph (b1918). Few American architects can match the virtuosity of this architect or his skilful treatment of form. In this highly modelled university building, he first employed a heavily corrugated concrete finish which was to be widely imitated. The result is like a sophisticated Le Corbusier, whose presence can be felt.

BELOW Marin County Civic Center, California, USA (1959–62). Wright's last great work, completed after his death. Here his long-established love of horizontal form was concentrated to weld the building massively into the landscape. If it looks today like a space vehicle, this is because science fiction has borrowed from the architect, and not the other way round.

LEFT Pirelli Building, Milan, Italy (1955–58). Gio Ponti (1891–1979). An elegant tower by one of Italy's most sophisticated artists, equally accomplished as a furniture designer and painter. The tapered profile was made possible by a structural core of reinforced concrete by Nervi.

BELOW Palazzetto dello Sport, Rome (Nervi, 1959). One of the two magnificent stadia built for the Olympics by Italy's foremost engineer.

BOTTOM Hunstanton School, Norfolk, England (Smithsons, 1954). The introduction of New Brutalism came when the Smithsons won this school in competition. All building elements and services were openly expressed, an approach predating the "Boilerhouse" school of the 1970s.

LEFT Engineering Faculty, Leicester University (James Stirling, 1959–63). Stirling's choice of a tower to house laboratories and workshops was an unconventional one, but the extensive industrial glazing was a practical way to provide maximum lighting.

■ 1970s and post-modernism

Post-Modernism arose out of a general worldwide loss of confidence in the International Modern Movement and a realization of its inadequacies. People were becoming bored and alienated by the severe cubic shapes and abstract geometry of Modernism. It was too uniform and lacked any sort of historical reference which could provide a feeling of continuity – an idea of place, time and, above all, identity. After this severity the public was ready for more variety, it wanted signs of individuality and even frivolity.

The 1980 exhibition 'The Presence of the Past' – as part of the Venice Biennale – encapsulated the feelings and style of the movement in the main exhibit, the *Strada Nuovissima*. This was a street consisting of 20 facades which had been designed by, among others, Robert Venturi, Charles Moore, Ricardo Bofill, Hans Hollein and Leon Krier. This "street" contained some of the design characteristics now commonly associated with Post-Modernism, in particular Classical orders used in an exaggerated playful way.

This playfulness is important to the movement. Post-Modernism has been described as theatrical and kitschy; it is also said to be trying to create instant or neo-History. Indeed its practitioners do employ columns, pediments and rustication as a sort of "coding". The use of gaudy colours – especially primary ones – is all part of the lack of seriousness. For example in some buildings the Classical orders are there, but are made from such materials as neon or bright metal. On the AT&T headquarters in New York (1978–84) by Philip Johnson – considered by many to be the high priest of Post-Modernism – the broken pediment in the Chippendale style on top of the skyscraper seems to be part of a private joke – a joke which has been so widely copied that it has become a cliché.

In Europe, the Post-Modern spirit is encapsulated in Taller (meaning "studio") de Arquitectura by Ricardo Bofill. Les Espaces d'Abraxus (1978–84) is a housing development in the new town of Marne-la-Vallée, 10 miles outside Paris. Made up of three blocks – Theatre, Palace and Triumphal Arch – the design draws upon Classicism with columns and pilasters, yet uses the latest engineering techniques and materials, such as pre-cast concrete, to create a massive stage set, with the development's residents as the cast.

Perhaps the extreme example of Post-Modernist architecture is the Piazza d'Italia in New Orleans, Louisiana. Designed by the arch-exponent of the style, Charles Moore, between 1975 and 1980 for the local Italian community, it has as its focal point a fountain in the shape of Italy, with water running down along the rivers Po, Tiber and Arno. Moore has used each of the five Italian orders and, in the manner of medieval craftsman has incorporated his face on one wall of the fountain, spouting water from the mouth. The materials he has used include marble, stainless steel, neon and brick, and the overall effect is that of a brightly lit and painted ruined temple dedicated to some god of mischief or chaos.

There is much in this architecture to enjoy, and no Ruskin or Gropius has emerged to wag a finger, even if it were to be heeded any longer. The public failure of modern architecture has at least forced architects to turn a critical eye inwards on themselves. They can no longer impose alien environments. If they do, the results are vandalism or prettification. The first change in most sold-off state housing is to the front door: the desire for individuality, however conformist in itself, has not yet been squashed.

ABOVE Pennzoil Place, Houston, Texas (Philip Johnson and John Burgee, 1974–5). Anonymous wedge shapes proclaim corporate power.

RIGHT Mother's House, Philadelphia (Robert Venturi, 1962–4). One of the first buildings to make the bold move from the cubes and right angles.

LEFT World Trade Center, New York (Yamasaki & Roth, 1962–77). These famous twin towers now dominate lower Manhattan, impressive by their size and by the magical way they catch the low sun of dawn and sunset. Architecturally they border on the dull and become oppressive close to.

ABOVE National Gallery, Washington DC (Pei, 1978). A difficult triangular site on which to build this gallery extension. Pei solved the problem brilliantly with this simple but sculptural wedge.

RIGHT AND BELOW Loyola Law School, Los Angeles, USA (Frank Gehry & Associates, 1981). Classical forms are here reduced and splintered into children's building blocks, whose wit disguises the underlying seriousness. Nevertheless, the effect is at once both disquieting and entertaining. A street view of the school shows the chapel; the building on the left is part of the old complex. The skylight to the chapel fails to respect the geometry of the roof — a deliberate, if uncomfortable mannerism.

LEFT House at New Castle, Delaware, USA (1978). Venturi has used cut-out early Doric or Cretan columns as symbolic substitutes for genuine structural members, brutally amputating one side just in case it might be misconstrued. The ambiguity and metaphor is both calculated and serious.

ABOVE AT&T headquarters, New York (Philip Johnson, 1978–84). This was the building which brought Post-Modernism to the attention of the world. Its broken pediment has now been so widely copied that it has become a cliché.

■ latest trends

After the economic recession of the 1970s, when many large building projects suffered, some indeed were abandoned, the 1980s saw a resurgence. In France the President Francois Mitterand instigated a series of spectacular projects which would leave a physical reminder of his administration for posterity. In Britain, London's Docklands became the largest building site in Europe and in the United States various imaginative schemes were launched to regenerate inner city areas and city centres.

Various new patrons also appeared on the scene anxious to encourage the new talent and vibrancy. While private or individual patronage had all but disappeared (apart from a few brave entrepreneurs such as Peter Palumbo in Britain), companies such as Sainsbury's in Britain and Doug Tompkins' Esprit in the United States became keen to be associated with the new architecture. Esprit used, among others, Shiro Kuromata, Jo D'urso, Ettore Sottsass and Norman Foster, and Sainsbury's caused some controversy with the choice of architects such as Nicholas Grimshaw whose "high tech" work many felt was not in keeping with food retailing. But as Richard Rogers said: "Modern architecture cannot be separated from modern life – it is part of life."

High Tech architecture has been described as the second machine aesthetic by architectural critic Charles Jencks. And while many high tech buildings owe a great deal more to the futurist visions of the 1960s "pop" architecture group Archigram, which put forward plans for "walking" and "plug-in" cities, the movement was foreshadowed by almost 100 years by the Eiffel Tower in Paris. For the ideas behind the Eiffel Tower (which caused a storm of protest in its day) and a high tech building such as the Pompidou Centre (another Parisian building to cause a storm), are patently similar. In both structures the skeleton of the building is on display, both are celebrations of technology.

That does not mean to say that the technology used is necessarily more advanced than that used in any other recent architectural movement, just that it is put on display and used to give the building a framework and character. In nearly all High Tech architecture this framework is deliberately designed to be flexible, so that the buildings can be either added to or reduced. For example, Norman Foster's Renault Building in Swindon (1982) consists of an aluminium-skinned series of canopies made up of yellow steel masts with cables extending out to struts. The whole structure can be dismantled or added to, to provide more storage, office or exhibition space.

In the case of Richard Rogers' and Renzo Piano's Pompidou Centre (1971–1977) the internal spaces can be altered – in their own words, they wanted: "A giant Meccano set rather than a traditional, static, transparent or solid doll's house."

The Hongkong & Shanghai Bank in Hong Kong (1979–86) by Norman Foster has been called the ultimate High Tech building. On a prime water-front site, it is made up of three slabs, all at different heights, so that although it looks like a solid rectangle from the front, from the side it looks rather like a fairy-tale castle with thin towers like pinnacles soaring to the sky. The bank has an atrium at its core and

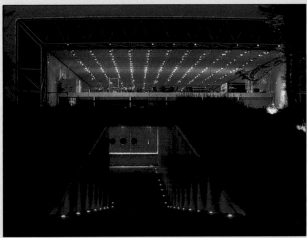

TOP Pompidou Centre, Paris (Renzo Piano and Richard Rogers, 1971–7). A people's palace whose popular success confounded its critics.

ABOVE Sainsbury Centre for the Visual Arts, Norwich, England (Foster Associates, 1977). Foster conceived this gallery as a vast hangar in an open field site. The night view shows the essentially simple space and industrial structure.

ABOVE Lloyds Building, London (1986). Richard Rogers (b1933). Rogers created this inside-out, technological framework in the new Lloyds Building. This controversial building is basically a large atrium around which the services, lifts and staircases — traditionally placed inside a building — are externally expressed.

LEFT Hongkong & Shanghai Bank, Hong Kong (Foster Associates, 1981–85). Foster is never architecturally incoherent and his technological bias is always classically handled. In this vast skyscraper, the vertebrate skeleton is boldly and effectively exposed, giving great visual and structural confidence.

throughout the inside of the building the X-shaped struts or trusses provide a strong motif as well as a reminder of its construction.

One of the most recently opened High Tech buildings is by Richard Rogers — who was once in partnership with Foster. It is the Lloyd's Building in London (1978–86). Although in the heart of the City, it does not attempt to blend in with any of the surrounding buildings but instead stands out with its "inside out" construction. Rogers has put all the services into towers which surround, but are separated from, the main building with its central atrium; this atrium, which goes the full height of the building, provides a central core around which the offices are grouped — from the outside it looks like a Victorian conservatory — and provides an amusing and effective contrast to the rest of the façade. Although a concrete construction, the façade is surfaced with steel and glass which, with all the services on the outside, creates a glittering surface by day and a dramatic silhouette by night.

Norman Foster's earlier Sainsbury Centre For The Visual Arts at the University of East Anglia, UK (1978) also has a glass and metal exterior, yet this early High Tech building has avoided putting all its working parts on display by creating a double-skin to contain all the pipes as well as to provide insulation; the result is very sleek and delicate, while still remaining distinctly High Tech.

glossary

abacus Flat piece at the top of a capital.

acropolis. Greek citadel sited prominently above the rest of a city.

agora Greek forum or market-place.

aisle Subsidiary part of a church or other large building parallel to the main body of the buildling.

ambulatory Internal extension to a circular or semicircular building; often forms the east end of a cathedral.

apse Semicircular recessed end to a church sanctuary or chapel.

arcade Corridor of arches on piers or columns.

architrave Lowest of the three main parts of an entablature. Also, the moulded frame around a door or window.

axonometric projection Geometrical drawing in three dimensions.

balcony Platform extension to a wall.

baldacchino Canopy over a throne or altar.

baluster Pillar or column supporting a handrail or coping.

Baroque In architecture, a mainly 17th-century late Renaissance style of flowing forms, exuberant decoration and complex spatial compositions.

barrel vault Semicircular arch, ceiling or roof; simplest type of vault.

basilica In Roman and early Christian architecture, a rectangular building supported internally with double colonnades and with a semicircular apse at one end.

Bauhaus German design school founded in Weimar in 1906 and named by Walter Gropius in 1919. Its philosophy was austere functionalism – no ornamentation – and the use of industrial materials and inter-disciplinary methods and techniques.

beton brut State of concrete once any casting framework has been removed.

Brutalism Functionalist style of the 1950s–60s that left materials such as concrete determinedly undisguised.

buttress Supportive wall of brick or stone.

campanile Freestanding bell-tower, particularly in Italy.

cantilever Any structural part of a building that projects beyond its support and overhangs.

capital Top of a column or pilaster.

caryatid Supportive column carved in the shape of a female figure.

centering Wooden frame supporting an arch or dome during construction.

chancel Choir and altar area of a church.

Chicago School Number of architects in late 19th-century Chicago who pioneered skyscrapers.

cladding Protective screen or covering on the outside of a building.

clapboard Overlapping horizontal boards protecting the outside of a house.

Classical architecture Form of style devised by the Greeks and Romans and revived during the Renaissance.

Classical orders Three main styles in the design of a column and its entablature: Corinthian, Ionic and Doric.

clerestory (clearstorey) Wall above supportive columns that is pierced by windows.

cloisters Roofed passage between a chapel of a monastery and the monks' quarters.

coffer Decorative recessed panel in a ceiling.

collar Horizontal beam in a timber roof linking the rafters and so forming an A-shaped truss.

colonnade Row of columns.

Constructivism Post-World War I Russian art style emphasizing abstract aspects of composition and design using industrial materials and methods.

coping Protective capping or covering on the top of a wall.

corbel Brick or stone block projecting from a wall to support a beam.

Corinthian order Most complex – most decorated – of the Classical orders.

cornice Projecting moulding running along the top of a building, an arch or a column.

cross-vault Arch made by two barrel vaults at right-angles to each other, meeting in the middle. Also called a groin-vault.

crucks Pairs of large curved beams used as the principal framework members of English houses until the 16th century.

curtain wall Thin protective external wall in front of the main frame of a building, now usually made of glass and light metals.

Dadaism Anti-art-establishment movement of the early 20th century that had little direct influence on architecture.

Deconstructivism Post-Modernist mainly US movement to banish formal preconceptions about building style while retaining modern building techniques and materials.

De Stijl Dutch geometric abstract movement emphasizing the unity of all the arts; named after a magazine, it above all gave a new dynamic to community housing projects.

Doric order Simplest – least decorated – of the three Classical orders.

drum Circular or polygonal wall that supports a dome.

dry joint Joint without mortar between the stones in a wall.

eaves Overhanging part underneath a sloping roof.

elevation Drawing of one aspect of a planned building in the vertical plane.

entablature Decorative mouldings above the top of a Classical column, comprising architrave, frieze and cornice.

entasis Convex curve in a column to correct for the optically concave effect of a column built straight.

Expressionism Inventive Germanic art and architecture movement emphasizing the notion of expressing an inner vision; results were sometimes fantastical.

faience Glazed earthenware often used as a decorative feature in a building.

fan vault Arched ceiling in which ribs radiate like a fan.

fenestration Windows and their arrangement in a building.

flying buttress Buttress in the form of an arch or half-arch, intended to support roof vaults laterally from outside a building.

formwork Timber or metal mould or casing to hold wet concrete until it dries. It is also known as shuttering.

frieze Decorated band either on the upper part of an internal wall or on an entablature.

functionalism Principle of the Modern Movement in architecture, that everything seen and used in building should have a function; no decoration for its own sake.

gable Triangular section of wall beneath the ridge of the roof, particularly over a window set vertically into the roof.

gallery Long thin room; also, in a church, an upper floor overlooking the nave.

geodesic dome Hemispherical dome made of prefabricated geometrically-shaped units interconnecting to give stability in all directions.

Gothic West European architectural style of the 12th–15th centuries, characterized by pointed arches. Aspects of the style were revived in later centuries.

groin-vault See **cross-vault**.

half-timbered Having a timber frame then filled around with rough material and plaster.

hammerbeam Short beam projecting near the top of a wall to support one of the rafters of the roof, making a tie-beam unnecessary.

hypostyle hall Grand hall in whch the roof is supported on pillars running the length of the central space.

infill Rough material, such as rubble, used to fill in a framework to create walls which are then finished with plaster or similar; also the insertion of new buildings between existing ones.

International (Modern) style US term referring to what in Europe was the Modern Movement of the early 20th century; the style featured undecorated cubic forms, white rendering and a horizontal aspect emphasized in large windows.

Ionic order Intermediate form of the three Classical orders.

joinery Making and fixing wood trimmings on a building.

lancet window Thin, pointed window typical of the Early English style of Gothic.

lantern Tower with a window on top of a dome.

load-bearing Weight-distributing and supporting.

loggia Gallery open or with a colonnade along one side.

machicolation On castle walls, an overhanging parapet with a hole in the floor through which molten lead or missiles could be dropped.

Mannerism In 16th-century Italy a style involving deliberate distortions of the traditional motifs in order to individualize the artist. In the 20th century, the attribution of importance to the manner in which something is done rather than to the meaning behind it.

Mansard roof Roof with a lower section sloping more steeply than an upper.

minaret Thin tall tower attached to a mosque, from which a muezzin calls the faithful to prayer.

Modern Movement Early 20th century European style which featured undecorated cubic forms, white rendering and a horizontal aspect emphasized in large windows.

Modulor Le Corbusier's system for establishing the proportions of building spaces corresponding to proportions of the male human body.

mortice and tenon Right-angled timber joint in which a projecting tenon is glued or pinned into a cut-away mortice.

motte and bailey Enclosure (bailey) surrounding an earthen mound (motte) as part of early defensive fortifications.

mouldings Ornamental trimmings added to flat surfaces, cornices and columns.

mullion Vertical spar dividing a window or any other opening.

nave Main body of a church.

neoprene gasket Strip of synthetic rubber into which window glazing is set to give a weatherproof seal.

organic In architecture, loosely based on natural physical structures.

oriel window Curved window projecting out of an upper storey.

pavilion Building, usually of light constructive materials, intended as a summerhouse.

pedestal Base of a column.

pediment In Classical style, the low-pitched gable above the entablature; since Renaissance times, any roof end.

pendentives Horizontal triangular constructions at the top of a square or rectangular building that allow a dome to be set centrally above.

peristyle Surrounding colonnade.

piano nobile Main floor of a house, one storey above the ground, containing the reception rooms that have higher ceilings than rooms on other floors.

piazza Public square in Italy.

pilaster Supportive column, generally of one of the three Classical orders, that projects from a wall.

pilotis Constructional "stilts" that support a building, leaving parking space or pedestrian access beneath; the form was pioneered by Le Corbusier.

pitched roof Roof of two planes sloping to a central ridge.

podium Platform supporting more than one column.

portico Grand entrance, having its own roof supported on at least one side by columns.

post-and-beam Comprising vertical posts supporting horizontal beams; another term for this is "trabeated"

Post-Modern Contemporary form of architecture, described as "more a spirit than a style", that features especially patterned brickwork, pitched roofs, turrets and round windows.

pre-stressed concrete Specially strengthened concrete to which steel wires under tension are added while the concrete is still wet; the tension is released once the concrete is set, giving yet further inherent strength.

quoin Dressed stone at the corner of a building.

reinforced concrete Concrete that is strengthened by the insertion of rods of steel, wire mesh or strands of glass-reinforced plastic or similar materials.

rendering Applying a smooth finish of plaster or stucco or similar material.

Renaissance In architecture, of the revival of Greek and Roman architectural principles and their reinterpretation, beginnng in Italy during the 15th and 16th centuries.

rib Projecting band across a ceiling or vault, generally structural.

rib vault Cross-vaulting in which ribs cross on the diagonal.

Rococo Final phase of Baroque style, involving light and often naturalistic ornamentation.

Romanesque Form of architecture after the Romans but before Gothic, thus between the 8th and 12th centuries, characterized by the semicircular (Roman) arch.

roof light Fixed or opening window in a roof.

rose window Round window in a frame of heavy tracery radiating out like the spokes of a wheel, and containing stained glass.

rotunda Round building, sometimes enclosed in a colonnade; also, a round room.

roughcast Covered in a rough material such as pebbledash.

sarsen stone Sandstone boulder.

scotia Concave moulding at the base of a column that casts a strong shadow.

services Facilities that have to be planned within a building to make living in it comfortable: heating and air-conditioning pipes and vents, electrical and telephone wiring ducts, water and sanitation amenities, and so forth.

shingle style Late 19th-century US style involving cladding houses with shingles, or wooden tiles, over timber frames.

shuttering See **formwork**.

skin In architecture, the outer membrane of a building: the brick walls, glass and steel cladding, and so on.

space frame construction The use of high-tech materials to construct buildings which enclose large areas without internal support; tension and elasticity are the principles mostly involved.

spandrel Triangular section of masonry above the junction of two arches in sequence.

stepped gable Particularly Dutch form of gable with stepped sides.

strapwork Elizabethan decoration on ceilings and screens that looks rather like cut leather.

string course Projecting band of stone, brick or other moulding running horizontally along the face of a building.

stucco Form of plaster.

tensile structures See **space frame construction**.

trabeated See **post-and-beam**.

tracery Ornamental stone framework, generally carved in sections.

transept Either of the "arms" of a cross-shaped church.

transom Horizontal bar across a window or panel.

truss Individual section of supportive framework bridging a space.

vault Arched ceiling or roof, usually in brick or stone.

vernacular In architecture, of traditional and indigenous historical style.

volumetric Relating to the three-dimensional qualities of a space.

volute Spiral scroll carved on the capital of an Ionic column.

voussoir Wedge-shaped block, one of a number used to form an arch.

index
· · · · · · · · ·

Notes

1. *Italicised* numbers refer to captions for illustrations. There are usually also textual references on these pages.
2. Where there are several entries the major reference is shown in **bold** numbers. This also indicates illustrations in most cases.
3. Only buildings that have been *illustrated* or mentioned more than once have been included.

acknowledgements

Michael Freeman: Jacket photograph, p 12 l. **Ronald Sheridan's Photo Library:** pp 6; 9; 12 c; 12 r; 80 bl; 80/81 c. **Andrew Higgot:** pp 8; 99 l, r; 102; 103; 112 t; 122 t; 122 bl. **Architectural Press:** p 7. **C C Handisyde:** p 11 t. **Simon Hudspith:** p 11 b. **Trewin Copplestone:** pp 13; 22 b; 33; 38 l; 60 c, cl, tr; 61 t; 69 c; 69 l; 71 t; 76 t; 77 l, c; 90; 91; 96 b; 97; 133 b. **British Tourist Authority:** p 15. **Mary Parsons:** p 16 l. **Robert Vickery:** pp 16 tr; 111; 115. **Brick Development Association:** p 16 br. **Paul Oliver:** p 18. **Richard Rogers Partnership:** p 19 t. **Andrew Holmes:** p 19 b. **Architectural Association:** pp 20; 24 l; 98 l; 113; 129 b; 134 l; 93 t. **D. Plummer:** p 21 t. **Bastian Valkenburg:** p 21 b. **James Sterling:** p 22 t. **Picturepoint:** pp 23 t; 50 l. **Design Aspect:** pp 24 r; 85 l. **Peter Mackertitch:** p 25 t. **Roy Summers:** p 25 b; 96 t. **Ricard Bryant:** p 26. **Canon Parsons:** pp 30; 40 l; 44; 47; 48; 49; 55; 63 br; 82; 93 b. **Sonia Halliday:** p 34; 37 t; 42 tl. **Anthony Hamber:** pp 37; 63 tl; 71 b; 73. **Philip Heather:** p 38 l. **Edwin Smith:** p 39. **George Michell:** p 41. **Bruce Coleman:** p 42 bl. **D Branch:** p 43 r. **Nick Clarke:** pp 45; 46; 53. **England Scene:** p 50 r. **A Tabbara:** pp 52; 70. **Colin Penn:** p 54. **Theo Armour:** p 60 br. **Alan Blanc:** p 61 b. **Tim Bidwell:** p 62 t. **Jessica Dunham:** p 62 r. **Hazel Cook:** pp 66; 75; 76 b; 116 t. **Bernard Cox:** pp 67 t; 133 l. **Peter Cook:** p 68. **E A Fleming-Hewett:** p 69 br. **Tadeus Barucki:** p 72 t. **Charles Jencks:** pp 72 c; b; 134 l. **Valerie Bennet:** pp 74 tl, c; 78 l, r; 138 r. **Marjorie Morrison:** p 74 b. **James Bogle:** p 77 r. **Barry Capper:** p 79 t. **Stephen Griffith:** p 79 c. **Sir John Summerson:** p 79 b. **Philpotts:** p 80 l. **H T Cadbury Brown:** pp 83; 125. **Liam O'Connor:** p 84. **Mary Anne Kennedy:** pp 65 r; 98 tr. **E R Jarrett:** pp 86/87; 101. **Angelo Hornak:** pp 88; 106; 119 b; 123; 125; 126; 129 t; 137 t;. **P Green:** p 89. **Ethel Hurwicz:** p 93 c. **Colin Penn:** p 94. **Peter Collmore:** pp 99 b; 127 b. **A F Kersting:** p 95. **Rosemary Ind:** p 100 tl. **Michael Ventris:** p 100 bl. **Polly Powell:** pp 104; 118. **David Carnwath:** pp 108 l; 116 c r. **Ed Teitelman:** 107 t, b; 109 110; 111; 117; 124; 128 b. **Nicholas Boyarsky:** p 108 r. **Mark Mucassey:** p 110. **Julian Feary:** p 112 b. **Norman Reuter:** p 116 br. **D. Wild ;** p 116 l. **Stuart Myers:** p 122 tr. **R Webster:** p 127 t. **Adrian Gale:** p 127 c. **Clive Pascall:** pp 130/131 b. **Henry Urena:** p 131 tl. **Geoffry Smythe:** p131 c. **Ingrid Morris:** p 131 tr. **Univerity of Leicester:** p 132. **Brian Westwood:** p 133r. **J Lynfield:** p 135 r. **Dennis Crompton:** 136 t. **Clinton Terry:** 136 b. **Vernon Gibberd:** p 137 b. **Ken Kirkwood:** p 138 l. **Dave Burton:** p 138 t. **Norman Foster and Associates:** p 139.